English Grammar for Students of German

W9-AWG-665

The Study Guide
for Those Learning German

Fifth edition

Cecile Zorach
Franklin and Marshall College

Charlotte Melin
University of Minnesota

Elizabeth A. Kautz
University of Minnesota

The Olivia and Hill Press®

THE O&H STUDY GUIDES
Jacqueline Morton, editor

English Grammar for Students of French
English Grammar for Students of Spanish
English Grammar for Students of German
English Grammar for Students of Italian
English Grammar for Students of Latin
English Grammar for Students of Russian
English Grammar for Students of Japanese
English Grammar for Students of Arabic
English Grammar for Students of Chinese
Gramática española para estudiantes de inglés

Printed in the U.S.A.

ISBN: 978-0-934034-38-8

Library of Congress Control Number: 2008940972

CONTENTS

CONTENTS

CONTENTS

STUDY TIPS

English Grammar for Students of German explains the grammatical terms that are in your textbook and shows how they relate to English grammar. Once you understand the terms and concepts in your own language, it will be easier for you to understand and learn German grammar. To help you become a more efficient language learner, we offer specific study tips for learning different types of words.

STUDY GUIDE

Before doing an assignment — Read the sections in *English Grammar* that cover the topics you are going to study. On our website, www.oliviahill.com, you can find *Correlations* to popular college textbooks indicating the pages to be read in preparation for each German grammar point introduced in class.

Homework — Take notes as you study your textbook. Highlighting is not sufficient. The more often you write down and use vocabulary and rules, the easier it will be for you to remember them. Complete exercises and activities over several short periods of time rather than in one long session. Don't get behind. You need time to absorb the material and to develop the skills.

Written exercises — As you write German words or sentences, say them out loud. Each time you write, read, say, and hear a word it reinforces it in your memory.

In class — Take notes. When your teacher gives you a new example or you hear a phrase while watching a video program, write it down so that you can analyze it. Once you have mastered a new concept, make up simple statements. Begin by modeling your sentences after the examples in your textbook. Later you will be able to express your own ideas.

Objective — Your aim is to be able to communicate correctly in German, orally and in writing, without reference to a textbook or dictionary. The *Study Tips* below and throughout this handbook will help you with this learning process.

TIPS FOR LEARNING VOCABULARY

One aspect of language learning is remembering many foreign words.

Remembering German words — Below are suggestions to help you associate a German word with an English word with a similar meaning. This is the first step and it will put the German word in your short-term memory. Use and practice, the next step, will put the words in your long-term memory.

1. Sometimes words are easy to learn because they are the same or very similar in both English and German. These words are easy to recognize in German, but you will have to concentrate on the differences in spelling and pronunciation.

house	Haus
to swim	schwimmen
green	grün

2. Try to associate the German word with another German word that you already know.

Freund	freundlich	*friend, friendly*
abfahren	Abfahrt	*to depart, departure*
klein	verkleinern	*small, to reduce*

3. Group words by topics or personal associations — It is easier to learn new words if you group them according to themes such as food, clothing, sports, school, home, etc. Think about the different kinds of words you will need to communicate about a particular topic. Try to learn action and descriptive words along with the words for people, places, and things. For example, take the topic of your living situation. To create sentences, you need to know more than the words for furniture!

apartment	to rent	cheap, expensive
dorm	to live	clean, dirty
roommate	to share	friendly, nice

   You may also find it helpful to group words by category, such as opposites (big ≠ small, tall ≠ short).

4. To reinforce the German word and its spelling, use it in a short sentence.

Memorizing German words — Flashcards are a good, handy tool for learning new words and their meaning. You can carry them with you, group them as you wish and add information as you advance. Creating your own flashcards is an important first step in learning vocabulary.

1. Write the German word or expression on one side of an index card and its English equivalent on the other side.

2. On the German side add a short sentence using the word or expression. To make sure that your sentence is grammatically correct, copy an example from your textbook substituting the names of people and places with ones you know. It will make it easier for you to remember a word in a familiar context. For review purposes, note down the chapter and page number of your textbook where the word is introduced.

3. On the German side include any irregularities and whatever information is relevant to the word in question. You will find specific suggestions under the *Study Tips* sections of this handbook.

Using the flashcards — Regardless of the side you're working on, always say the German word out loud.

1. Look at the German side first. Going from German to English is easier than from English to German because it only requires your recognizing the German word. Read the German word(s) out loud, giving the English equivalent, then check your answer on the English side.

2. When you can go easily from German to English, turn the cards to the English side. Going from English to German is harder because you have to pull the word and its spelling out of your memory. Say the German equivalent out loud as you write it down, then check the spelling. Some students prefer closing their eyes and visualizing the German word and its spelling.

3. As you progress, put aside the cards you know and concentrate on the ones you still don't know.

TIPS FOR LEARNING WORD FORMS

Another aspect of language learning is remembering the various forms a word can take; for example, another form of *book* is *books* and *do* can take the form of *does* and *did*. As a general rule, the first part of the word indicates its meaning and the second part indicates its form.

Learning German forms — Paper and pencil are the best tools to learn the various forms of a word. You should write them down until you get them right. The following steps will make learning forms easier.

1. Look for a pattern in the different forms of a word.
   - Which letters, if any, remain constant?
   - Which letters change?

- Is there a pattern to the changes?
- Is this pattern the same as one you already know?
- If this pattern is similar to one you already know, what are the similarities and differences?

130

We will help you establish patterns in the *Study Tips* following selected chapters.

2. Once you have established the pattern, it will be easy to memorize the forms.

   - Take a blank piece of paper and write down the forms while saying them out loud.
   - Continue until you are able to write all the forms correctly without referring to your textbook.

3. Write short sentences using the various forms.

140

Reviewing German forms — You can use flashcards to review forms, not to learn them. You will find suggestions on what to write on the cards under the *Study Tips*.

LIST OF STUDY TIPS

WHAT'S IN A WORD?

When you learn a foreign language, in this case German, you must look at each word in four ways: MEANING, PART OF SPEECH, FUNCTION, and FORM.

MEANING

An English word may be connected to a German word that has a similar meaning.

> *Tree* has the same meaning as the German word **Baum.**

Words with equivalent meanings are learned by memorizing vocabulary (see pp. 1-3). There are many words, called COGNATES, that have the same meaning and approximately the same spelling in English and German.

Haus	*house*
Garten	*garden*
Student	*student*
intelligent	*intelligent*

Occasionally knowing one German word will help you learn another.

> Knowing that **Kellner** means *waiter* should help you learn that **Kellnerin** is *waitress*; or knowing that **wohnen** means *to live* and that **Zimmer** means *room* should help you learn that **Wohnzimmer** means *living room.*

However, there is usually little similarity between words, and knowing one German word will not help you learn another. In general, you must memorize each vocabulary item separately.

> Knowing that **Mann** means *man* will not help you learn that **Frau** means *woman.*

Words that have the same basic meaning in English and German rarely have identical meanings in all situations.

> The word **Mann** generally has the same meaning as *man*, but it can also mean *husband*. The word **Frau** usually means *woman*, but it can also mean *wife*, a married woman, *Mrs.*, or even *Ms.*

In addition, every language has its own phrases or way of expressing ideas; these are called IDIOMATIC EXPRESSIONS or IDIOMS.

1

10

20

30

The word *keep* has a special meaning in the expression *keep your fingers crossed*. The equivalent German expression is **die Daumen drücken** [word-for-word: press your thumbs].

You will have to be on the alert for these idioms because they cannot be translated word-for-word.

PART OF SPEECH

In English and German a word can be classified as belonging to one of eight categories called PARTS OF SPEECH.

noun	article
pronoun	adverb
verb	preposition
adjective	conjunction

Some parts of speech are further broken down according to type. Adjectives, for instance, can be descriptive, interrogative, demonstrative, or possessive. Each part of speech has its own rules for spelling, pronunciation, and use.

In order to choose the correct German equivalent of an English word, you must learn to identify its part of speech. For example, look at the word *plays* in the following sentences.

Axel *plays* soccer.

verb → **spielt**

Axel likes *plays*.

noun → **Schauspiele**

The English word is the same in both sentences. In German, however, different words are used, and different sets of rules apply, because each *plays* belongs to a different part of speech. The various sections of this handbook show you how to identify parts of speech so that you can choose the proper German words and the rules that apply to them.

FUNCTION

In English and German the role a word plays in a sentence is called its FUNCTION. Depending on the sentence, the same word can have a variety of functions.

subject
direct object
indirect object
object of a preposition

In order to choose the correct German equivalent of an English word, you must learn to identify its function.

For example, look at the word *her* in the following sentences.

I don't know *her*.

direct object → **sie**

Have your told *her* your story?

indirect object → **ihr**

The English word is the same in both sentences. In German, however, different words are used, and different sets of rules apply, because each *her* has a different function. The various sections of this handbook show you how to identify the function of words so that you can choose the proper German words and the rules that apply to them.

FORM

In English and in German, a word can influence the form of another word, that is, its spelling and pronunciation. This "matching" is called AGREEMENT and it is said that one word "agrees" with another.

I am   *am* agrees with *I*
she is   *is* agrees with *she*

Agreement does not play a big role in English, but it is an important part of the German language. For example, look at the sentences below where the lines indicate which words must agree with one another.

*The blue **book** is on the big old table.*

Das blaue **Buch** ist auf dem großen alten **Tisch**.

In English, the only word that affects another word in the sentence is *book*, which causes us to say *is*. If the word were *books,* we would have to say *are*. In German, the word for *book* (**Buch**) not only affects the word for *is* (**ist**), but also the spelling and pronunciation of the German words for *the* (**das**) and *blue* (**blaue**). The words for *is on* (**ist auf**) and *table* (**Tisch**) affect the spelling and pronunciation of the equivalent words for *the* (**dem**), *big* (**großen**), and *old* (**alten**). The only word not affected by the words surrounding it is the word for *on* (**auf**).

As the various parts of speech are introduced in this handbook, we will go over "agreement" so that you learn which words agree with others and how the agreement is shown.

CHAPTER

WHAT IS A NOUN?

A **NOUN** is a word that can be the name of a person, animal, place, thing, event, or idea.

■ a person	friend, sister, student, gardener, doctor, Jacob, Katie, Professor Meyer
■ an animal	dog, falcon, fish, bear, Snoopy, Fluffy, Mickey Mouse
■ a place	stadium, restaurant, city, state, country, Zurich, Bavaria, New York, Austria, Europe
■ a thing	desk, house, border, water, hand, Monday, White House, Volkswagen
■ an event or activity	birth, graduation, jogging, growth, the Olympics, Thanksgiving
■ an idea or concept	truth, poverty, peace, fear, beauty, time, humor, justice, hatred

As you can see, a noun is not only a word that names something that is tangible (i.e., something you can touch), such as *desk, restaurant,* or *White House,* it can also be the name of something that is abstract (i.e., that you cannot touch), such as *truth, peace,* and *humor.*

A noun that is the name of a specific person, place, or thing, etc. is called a **PROPER NOUN**. A noun that does not state the name of specific person, place, or thing, etc. is called a **COMMON NOUN**.

Ingrid is my friend.
proper   common
noun   noun

A noun made up of two or more words is called a **COMPOUND NOUN**. A compound noun may be made up of two common nouns written as one word *(snowball),* as two words *(school year),* or with a hyphen *(self-interest).* It can also be a combination of a common noun and other parts of speech such as *Civil War* and *Berlin Wall.*

IN ENGLISH

Proper nouns always begin with a capital letter. Common nouns, however, only begin with a capital letter when they are the first word of a sentence or question.

To help you learn to recognize nouns, look at the para- [40]
graph below where the nouns are in *italics*.

The *United States* imports many *items* from German-
speaking *countries*. German *automobiles*, ranging from
moderately priced *models* to elegant *cars*, have earned a
reputation here for their excellent *performance*. *Germany*
also supplies us with fine *tools, cameras,* and *electronics*.
Many *Americans* value *watches* imported from *Switzer-
land*. Nearly everyone in our *country* appreciates the
taste of Swiss *chocolate*.

[50]

IN GERMAN

Nouns are identified the same way as they are in English.
In German, however, they are very easy to recognize since
all nouns, proper and common, are capitalized, regardless
of where they are in a sentence.

TERMS USED TO TALK ABOUT NOUNS

- **Gender** — In German, a noun has a gender; that is, it can
  be classified according to whether it is masculine, feminine, or neuter (see *What is Meant by Gender?*, p. 10). [60]

- **Number** — A noun has number; that is, it can be identified
  as being singular or plural (see *What is Meant by Number?*,
  p. 14).

- **Function** — A noun can have a variety of functions in a
  sentence; that is, it can be the subject of the sentence (see
  What is a Subject?, p. 41), a predicate noun (see *What is a
  Predicate Noun?*, p. 44), or an object (see *What is an Object?*,
  p. 53).

- **Case** — In German, a noun can have a variety of forms
  depending on its function in the sentence (see *What is* [70]
  Meant by Case?, p. 35).

WHAT IS MEANT BY GENDER?

1   **GENDER** in the grammatical sense means that a word can be classified as masculine, feminine, or neuter.

> Did Franz give Ingrid the book? Yes, *he* gave *it* to *her*.
>   masc. neuter fem.

Grammatical gender is not very important in English. However, it is at the very heart of the German language where the gender of a word is often reflected not only in the way the word itself is spelled and pronounced, but also in the way all
10   the words connected to it are spelled and pronounced.

More parts of speech indicate gender in German than in English.

ENGLISH	GERMAN
pronouns	nouns
possessive adjectives	articles
	pronouns
	adjectives

Since each part of speech follows its own rules to indicate gender, you will find gender discussed in the sections dealing
20   with articles and with the various types of pronouns and adjectives. In this section we shall look at the gender of nouns only.

IN ENGLISH

Nouns themselves do not have gender, but sometimes their meaning indicates a gender based on the biological sex of the person or animal the noun represents. For example, when we replace a proper or common noun that refers to one man or woman, we use *he* for males and *she*
30   for females.

- nouns referring to males indicate the **MASCULINE** gender

> Lukas came home; *he* was happy; the dog was glad to see *him*.
> noun (male)   masculine   masculine

- nouns referring to females indicate the **FEMININE** gender

> Anja came home; *she* was happy; the dog was glad to see *her*.
> noun (female)   feminine   feminine

All the proper or common nouns that are not perceived as having a biological gender are considered NEUTER and are replaced by *it* when they refer to one thing, place, or idea.

The city of Munich is lovely. I enjoyed visiting *it*.
     | |
  noun   neuter

IN GERMAN

All nouns—common nouns and proper nouns—have a gender; they are masculine, feminine, or neuter. Do not confuse the grammatical terms "masculine" and "feminine" with the terms "male" and "female." Only a few German nouns have a grammatical gender tied to whether they refer to someone of the male or female sex; most nouns have a gender that must be memorized.

The gender of most German nouns cannot easily be explained or figured out. These nouns have a grammatical gender that is unrelated to biological gender. Here are some examples of English nouns classified under the gender of their German equivalent.

MASCULINE	FEMININE	NEUTER
table	lamp	window
heaven	hope	girl
state	Switzerland	Germany
beginning	reality	topic

Textbooks and dictionaries usually indicate the gender of a noun with an *m.* for masculine, an *f.* for feminine, or *n.* for neuter. Sometimes the definite articles are used: **der** for masculine, **die** for feminine, or **das** for neuter (see *What is an Article?*, p. 17).

A German noun will usually have different forms when it refers to the different sexes. For example, the noun *student* has two equivalents, a feminine form **Studentin** for females and a masculine form **Student** for males.

As you learn a new noun, you should always learn its gender because it will affect the form of the words related to it.

CAREFUL — Do not rely on biological gender to indicate the grammatical gender of German nouns that can refer to either a male or a female. For instance, the grammatical gender of the nouns **Kind** *(child)* and **Baby** *(baby)* is always neuter, even though the person being referred to could be male or female.

Flashcards

1. Make a flashcard for each noun. You can do this by hand, or use a free online tool (simply search for "flash card maker"). Most online tools allow you to type in the information, practice with the cards online, and/or print out paper cards. For those with access to a Macintosh computer, consider making flashcards using Provoc (www.arizona-software.ch/provoc). This free software allows you to move your flashcards onto an iPod for vocabulary practice on the go!

2. Use either colored paper or a highlighter to color code the flashcards based on the gender of the noun: masculine = blue, feminine = red, neuter = green. Associating the noun with blue, red, or green will help you remember its gender.

3. On one side, write the German noun, including the singular article (see *What is an Article?*, p. 17). On the other side, write the word in English or use an image to depict the noun. You can find small images online at The Internet Picture Dictionary (www.pdictionary.com/german), or photos of objects in a German setting at the Culturally Authentic Pictorial Lexicon (www.washjeff.edu/CAPL).

Pattern

Gender can sometimes be determined by looking at the ending of the German noun. Here are some common endings you will want to notice.

MASCULINE ENDINGS

- nouns referring to male persons that end in **-er, -ist, -ling, -ent**

der Physiker	*the physicist*
der Pianist	*the pianist*
der Jüngling	*the young man*
der Student	*the student*

- names of seasons (except **das Frühjahr**, *spring*), months, days, parts of days (except **die Nacht**, *night*), geographical directions, and weather phenomena

der Sommer	*summer*
der Januar	*January*
der Montag	*Monday*
der Mittag	*noon*
der Wind	*the wind*
der West	*west*

- most nouns which end in **-ig, -or, -ismus, -pf, -f**

der Pfennig	*the penny*
der Doktor	*the doctor*
der Optimismus	*optimism*
der Kopf	*the head*
der Senf	*mustard*

FEMININE ENDINGS
- most two-syllable nouns which end in -**e** (some common exceptions are **der Name,** *the name,* **der Käse,** *the cheese,* **das Auge,** *the eye*)

die Lampe	*the lamp*
die Seife	*the soap*

- nouns referring to female persons which end in -**in**

die Studentin	*the female student*
die Professorin	*the female Professor*

- nouns which end in -**ei,** -**ie,** -**heit,** -**keit,** -**schaft,** -**ung,** -**ion,** -**tät,** -**ur,** -**ik,** -**a**

die Bücherei	*library*
die Drogerie	*drugstore*
die Dummheit	*stupidity*
die Möglichkeit	*possibility*
die Freundschaft	*friendship*
die Prüfung	*test*
die Reaktion	*reaction*
die Universität	*university*
die Natur	*nature*
die Musik	*music*
die Pizza	*pizza*

NEUTER ENDINGS
- nouns ending in -**lein** or -**chen**

das Fräulein	*the young woman*
das Mädchen	*the young girl*

- nouns beginning with **Ge-**

das Gebäude	*the building*
das Gebet	*the prayer*

- verb infinitives used as nouns (gerunds, see p. 117-8)

das Lesen	*reading*
das Singen	*singing*

WHAT IS MEANT BY NUMBER?

NUMBER in the grammatical sense means that a word can be classified as singular or plural. When a word refers to one person or thing, it is said to be **SINGULAR**; when it refers to more than one, it is **PLURAL**.

one *book*   two *books*
| |
singular   plural

More parts of speech indicate number in German than in English, and there are also more spelling and pronunciation changes in German than in English.

ENGLISH	**GERMAN**
nouns	nouns
verbs	verbs
pronouns	pronouns
demonstrative adjectives	adjectives
	articles

Since each part of speech follows its own rules to indicate number, you will find number discussed in the sections dealing with articles, the various types of adjectives and pronouns, as well as in all sections on verbs and their tenses. In this section we will look at number in nouns only.

IN ENGLISH

A singular noun is made plural in one of two ways.

- a singular noun can add an "-s" or "-es"

   book book*s*
   kiss   kiss*es*

- a singular noun can change its spelling

   man m*en*
   leaf   lea*ves*
   child child*ren*

Some nouns, called **COLLECTIVE NOUNS**, refer to a group of persons or things, but the noun itself is considered singular.

   A soccer *team* has eleven players.
   My *family* is well.

IN GERMAN

As in English, the plural form of German nouns is often spelled differently, and therefore pronounced differently, from the singular form. German plurals, however, are less predictable than English plurals; there are more endings and more internal spelling changes than in English. As you learn new nouns in German, you should memorize each noun's gender (see *What is Meant by Gender?*, p. 10) and its singular and plural forms. In the examples below, notice that German often uses an **umlaut** (¨) to form plural nouns.

- the ending **-n** or **-en**

Auge	Augen	*eye*	*eyes*
Frau	Frauen	*woman*	*women*

- the ending **-e** (**umlaut** is sometimes added)

das Bein	die Beine	*leg*	*legs*
der Schuh	die Schühe	*shoe*	*shoes*

- the ending **-er** (**umlaut** added when the stem vowel is **a, o, u,** or **au**)

das Buch	die Bücher	*book*	*books*
das Haus	die Häuser	*house*	*houses*

- no ending (**umlaut** added when the stem vowel is **a, o, u,** or **au**)

der Lehrer	die Lehrer	*teacher*	*teachers*
der Vater	die Väter	*father*	*fathers*

STUDY TIPS — NOUNS AND THEIR NUMBER

Flashcards

Sort out the flashcards for nouns (see p. 12) and add the plural form of the noun, preceded by the definite article *(What is an Article?, p. 17).*

Patterns

Learning the plural forms of German nouns will be easier if you can determine some patterns.

1. Create a short list of nouns that have the same ending in the singular. Write down the plural form beside each noun.

GROUP 1		GROUP 2	
Prüf**ung**	Prüf**ung**en	Wint**er**	Wint**er**
Wohn**ung**	Wohn**ung**en	Zimm**er**	Zimm**er**
Zeit**ung**	Zeit**ung**en	Lehr**er**	Lehr**er**

What pattern do you see?
- nouns ending in **–ung** add **–en** in the plural.
- nouns ending in **–er** do not change in the plural.

2. Try to determine some patterns of number based on the gender of the noun. Create lists of feminine and masculine nouns. Write the plural form beside each noun.

FEMININE	PLURAL
Schule	Schulen
Tür	Türen
Freiheit	Freiheiten
Spezialität	Spezialitäten
Freundschaft	Freundschaften

MASCULINE	PLURAL
Lehrer	Lehrer
Freund	Freunde
Bruder	Brüder

What pattern do you see?

- feminine nouns often use **–n** or **–en** to form the plural.
- feminine nouns formed with suffixes, **-keit**, **–heit**, **-tät**, and **–schaft** use **–en** to form the plural.
- some masculine nouns do not have any ending in the plural.
- masculine nouns often use an umlaut and/or an **–e** to form the plural.

3. Paying attention to the ending of a German noun will provide you with clues to both its gender and how to form its plural. The plural form of one noun can help you remember the plural form of another noun with the same ending.

WHAT IS AN ARTICLE?

An **ARTICLE** is a word placed before a noun to show whether the noun refers to a specific person, animal, place, thing, event, or idea, or whether the noun refers to an unspecified person, thing, or idea.

> I saw *the* video you spoke about.
>
> a specific video
>
> I saw *a* video at school.
>
> an unspecified video

In English and in German, there are two types of articles, definite articles and indefinite articles.

DEFINITE ARTICLES
IN ENGLISH

A **DEFINITE ARTICLE** is used before a noun when we are speaking about a particular person, place, animal, thing, event, or idea. There is one definite article, *the*.

> I read *the* book you recommended.
>
> a specific book
>
> I ate *the* apple from your garden.
>
> a specific apple

The definite article remains *the* when the noun that follows becomes plural.

> I read *the books* you recommended.

IN GERMAN

As in English, a definite article is used before a noun when referring to a specific person, place, animal, thing, or idea.

> Ich aß **den Apfel** von deinem Garten.
> *I ate **the apple** from your garden.*

In German, the article works hand-in-hand with the noun to which it belongs in that it matches the noun's gender, number, and case. This "matching" is called **AGREEMENT** (one says that "the article *agrees* with the noun"). See *What is Meant by Gender?*, p. 10; *What is Meant by Number?*, p. 14; and *What is Meant by Case?*, p. 35.

A different definite article is used, depending on three factors.

40   1. GENDER — whether the noun is masculine, feminine, or neuter.

2. NUMBER — whether the noun is singular or plural.

3. CASE — the function of the noun in the sentence.

This chapter discusses only the basic form of the article as it is listed in the dictionary or in your textbook's vocabulary lists.

There are four forms of the definite article: three singular forms and one plural.

50   ▪ **der** indicates that the noun is masculine singular
   der Baum   ***the*** *tree*

▪ **die** indicates that the noun is feminine singular
   die Tür   ***the*** *door*

▪ **das** indicates that the noun is neuter singular
   das Haus   ***the*** *house*

▪ **die** is also the definite article for plural nouns
   die Türen   ***the*** *doors*

60   Since the same definite article **die** is used with plural nouns and with feminine singular nouns, you will have to rely on other indicators to determine the number of the noun. The most common indicator is the form of the noun itself: is it the singular form or the plural form?

die **Tür**
*the **door***

   Tür is a singular noun; therefore, **die** is feminine singular.

die **Türen**
*the **doors***

70   **Türen** is a plural noun; therefore, **die** is plural.

You will discover other indicators of number as you learn more German (see *What is a Verb Conjugation?*, p. 46).

INDEFINITE ARTICLES
IN ENGLISH

An indefinite article is used before a noun when we are speaking about an unspecified person, animal, place, thing, event, or idea. There are two indefinite articles, *a* and *an*.

- *a* is used before a word beginning with a consonant

    I saw *a* video at school.

    not a specific video

- *an* is used before a word beginning with a vowel or a vowel sound

    I ate *an* apple.

    not a specific apple

    She is taking *an* honors class.

    not a specific honors class

The indefinite article is used only with a singular noun; it is dropped when the noun becomes plural. At times the word *some* is used to replace it, but it is usually omitted.

    I saw videos at school.
    I saw *(some)* videos at school.

    I ate apples.
    I ate *(some)* apples.

IN GERMAN

As in English, an indefinite article is used before a noun when we are not speaking about a specific person, animal, place, thing, event, or idea. As in English, the indefinite article is used only with a singular noun. Just as with German definite articles, indefinite articles must agree with the noun in gender, number, and case. There are two forms of the indefinite article.

- **ein** indicates that the noun is masculine or neuter

    ein Baum   *a tree*

          masculine

    ein Haus   *a house*

          neuter

- **eine** indicates that the noun is feminine

    eine Tür   *a door*

          feminine

Your textbook will instruct you on the different forms of the definite and indefinite articles in greater detail.

Flashcards

1. Use your noun flashcards to memorize the meaning of the noun and the correct form of the definite article. As you look at the English side, say the definite article + noun out loud in German.
2. Repeat the above, this time using the plural definite article + the plural form of the noun.
3. Repeat the above, this time using the indefinite article + the singular form of the noun. Add an adjective such as **klein** *(small)* whose ending changes according to whether it precedes a masculine, feminine, or neuter noun. The change in ending of the adjective will reinforce the noun's gender in your memory.

ein kleiner Hund (m.)	*a small dog*
eine kleine Katze (f.)	*a small cat*
ein kleines Kind (n.)	*a small child*

CHAPTER

6

WHAT IS A PRONOUN?

A **PRONOUN** is a word used in place of one or more nouns. It may stand, therefore, for a person, place, thing, or idea. [1]

> *Karen* likes to sing. *She* practices every day.
> noun   pronoun

In the example above, the pronoun *she* refers to the proper noun *Karen* (see *What is a Noun?*, p. 8). A pronoun is always used to refer to someone or something that has already been mentioned. The word that the pronoun replaces is called the **ANTECEDENT** of the pronoun. *Karen* is the antecedent of the pronoun *she*. [10]

IN ENGLISH

There are different types of pronouns, each serving a different function and following different rules. The list below presents the most important types and refers you to the section where they are discussed.

PERSONAL PRONOUNS — These pronouns refer to different persons or things (i.e., *me, you, her, it*) and they change their form according to the function they have in a sentence (see p. 37). The personal pronouns include: [20]

Subject pronouns — These pronouns are used as the subject of a verb (see p. 42).

> *I* go.
> *They* read.
> *He* runs.

Object pronouns — These pronouns are used as:

- direct objects of a verb (see p. 57)

> Tina loves *him*.
> Mark saw *them* at the theater. [30]

- indirect objects of a verb (see p. 57)

> The boy wrote *me* the letter.
> Petra gave *us* the book.

- objects of a preposition (see p. 67)

> Angela is going to the movies with *us*.
> Don't step on it; walk around *it*.

REFLEXIVE PRONOUNS — These pronouns refer back to the subject of the sentence (see p. 141).

> I cut *myself.*
> She spoke about *herself.*

INTERROGATIVE PRONOUNS — These pronouns are used in questions (see p. 70).

> *Who* is that?
> *What* do you want?

POSSESSIVE PRONOUNS — These pronouns are used to show possession (see p. 81).

> Whose book is that? *Mine.*
> *Yours* is on the table.

RELATIVE PRONOUNS — These pronouns are used to introduce relative subordinate clauses (see p. 146).

> The man *who* came is very nice.
> Ingrid, *whom* you met, wants to study in Berlin.

IN GERMAN

Pronouns are identified in the same way as in English. The most important difference is that German pronouns have more forms than English pronouns since they must agree in gender, number, and case with the nouns they replace (see *What is Meant by Gender?*, p. 10, *What is Meant by Number?*, p. 14, and *What is Meant by Case?*, p. 35).

WHAT IS A PERSONAL PRONOUN?

A **PERSONAL PRONOUN** is a word used to refer to a person or thing that has previously been mentioned.

> Axel reads a book. *He* reads *it*.
>> *He* is a pronoun replacing a person, *Axel*.
>> *It* is a pronoun replacing a thing, *book*.

Personal pronouns can function as subjects, objects, and objects of prepositions. These functions are discussed in separate sections: *What is a Subject Pronoun?*, p. 42, *What are Direct and Indirect Object Pronouns?*, p. 57, and *What is an Object of Preposition Pronoun?*, p. 67.

In English and in German, personal pronouns, as well as other parts of speech, are often referred to by the **PERSON** to which they belong: 1st, 2nd, or 3rd, singular or plural. The word "person" in this instance is a grammatical term that does not necessarily mean a human being; it can also mean a thing.

IN ENGLISH

Each of the six "persons" is used to refer to one or more persons or things. We have listed them in the order they are usually presented and given the equivalent subject pronoun. Sometimes, as in the case of the 3rd person, more than one pronoun *(he, she,* and *it)* belongs to the same person.

1ST PERSON

I → person speaking → SINGULAR
we → person speaking plus others → PLURAL

> *Hans and I* are free this evening. *We* are going out.

2ND PERSON

you → person or persons spoken to → SINGULAR or PLURAL

> *Lukas,* do *you* sing folk songs?
> *Johan, Kurt and Tina,* do *you* sing folk songs?

3RD PERSON

he, she, it → person or object spoken about → SINGULAR
they → persons or objects spoken about → PLURAL

> *Tina and Axel* are free this evening. *They* are going out.

1

10

20

30

As you can see above, all the personal pronouns, except *you*, show whether one person or more than one is involved. For instance, the singular *I* is used by the person who is speaking to refer to himself or herself and the plural *we* is used by the person speaking to refer to himself or herself plus others. Let us look at each of these pronouns.

IN GERMAN

German personal pronouns are also identified as 1st, 2nd, and 3rd persons, each having a singular and a plural form. They are usually presented in the following order:

SINGULAR			
1st PERSON	*I*	ich	
2nd PERSON	*you*	du	FAMILIAR
		Sie	FORMAL
3rd PERSON	*he*	er	MASCULINE
	she	sie	FEMININE
	it	er	MASCULINE
		sie	FEMININE
		es	NEUTER
PLURAL			
1st PERSON	*we*	wir	
2nd PERSON	*you*	ihr	FAMILIAR
		Sie	FORMAL
3rd PERSON	*they*	sie	

CHOOSING THE CORRECT "PERSON"

Let us look at the English pronouns that have more than one equivalent in German: *you* and *it*.

"You"

IN ENGLISH

The same pronoun "you" is used to address one or more than one person.

> Ann, are *you* coming with me?
> Ann and Lukas, are *you* coming with me?

The same pronoun "you" is used to address anyone (person or animal), regardless of their rank.

> Do *you* have any questions, Mr. President?
> *You* are a good dog, Spot.

IN GERMAN

There are two sets of pronouns for *you*, the FAMILIAR FORM and the FORMAL FORM.

Familiar "you" → **du** or **ihr**

The familiar forms of *you* are used to address members of
one's family (notice that the word "familiar" is similar to
the word "family"), persons you call by their first name,
children and pets.

- to address one person (2ⁿᵈ person singular) → **du**

  Anja, are *you* there?
  |
  du

  Lukas, are *you* there?
  |
  du

- to address more than one person (2ⁿᵈ person plural) to
  whom you would say **du** individually → **ihr**

  Niko and Axel, are *you* there?
  |
  ihr

Formal "you" → **Sie**

The formal form of *you* is used to address persons you do
not know well enough to call by their first name or to
whom you should show respect (Ms. Smith, Mr. Jones, Dr.
Anderson, Professor Schneider). There is only one form,
Sie, regardless of whether you are addressing one or more
persons.

  Professor Schneider, are *you* there?
  |
  Sie

  Professor Schneider and Mrs. Schneider, are *you* there?
  |
  Sie

Note that the formal *you* form **Sie** is always capitalized. It
should help you distinguish it from **sie** the German pronouns for *she* and for *they*.

If in doubt as to whether to use the familiar or formal
form when addressing an adult, use the formal form. It
shows respect for the person you are talking to, and the
use of the familiar form might be considered rude.

"Iᴛ"

IN ENGLISH

Whenever you are speaking about one thing or idea, you
use the personal pronoun *it*.

  Where is the pencil? *It* is lying on the table.
  Kurt has an idea. *It* is very interesting.

IN GERMAN

The personal pronoun used depends on the gender of the German noun *it* replaces, its antecedent. Thus *it* can be either masculine, feminine, or neuter (see *What is Meant by Gender?*, p. 10).

To choose the correct form of *it*, you must identify two things:

1. ANTECEDENT — Find the noun *it* replaces.
2. GENDER — Determine the gender of the German word for the antecedent.

Here is an example for each gender.

- masculine antecedent → **er**

    *Where is the pencil? **It** is lying on the table.*
    ANTECEDENT: the pencil
    GENDER: **Der Bleistift** *(pencil)* is masculine.
    Wo ist der Bleistift? **Er** liegt auf dem Tisch.
    masculine

- feminine antecedent → **sie**

    *How was the trip? **It** was nice.*
    ANTECEDENT: the trip
    GENDER: **Die Reise** *(trip)* is feminine.
    Wie war die Reise? **Sie** war sehr schön.
    feminine

- neuter antecedent → **es**

    *Where is the book? **It** is on the table.*
    ANTECEDENT: the book
    GENDER: **Das Buch** *(book)* is neuter.
    Wo ist das Buch? **Es** ist auf dem Tisch.
    neuter

In both English and German personal pronouns have different forms to show their function in a sentence; these forms are called CASE FORMS (see *What is Meant by Case?*, p. 35).

7. STUDY TIPS — PERSONAL PRONOUNS

Flashcards

Make a flashcard for each personal pronoun, with a separate card for the four forms of *you*: singular familiar; singular formal; plural familiar; plural formal.

WHAT IS A VERB?

A **VERB** is a word that indicates the action of the sentence. The word "action" is used in its broadest sense; it is not necessarily a physical action.

Let us look at different types of words that are verbs.

- a physical activity   to run, to hit, to talk, to walk
- a mental activity   to hope, to believe, to imagine, to dream, to think
- a condition   to be, to have, to seem

Many verbs, however, do not fall neatly into one of the above three categories. They are verbs nevertheless because they represent the "action" of the sentence.

The book *costs* only $10.00.
      to cost

The table *seats* eight.
      to seat

The verb is the most important word in a sentence. You cannot write a **COMPLETE SENTENCE**, that is, express a complete thought, without a verb.

It is important to identify verbs because the function of a word in a sentence often depends on its relationship to the verb. For instance, the subject of a sentence is the word doing the action of the verb and the object is the word receiving the action of the verb (see *What is a Subject?*, p. 41, and *What is an Object?*, p. 53).

IN ENGLISH

To help you learn to recognize verbs, look at the paragraph below where the verbs are in italics.

The three students *entered* the restaurant, *selected* a table, *hung* up their coats and *sat* down. They *looked* at the menu and *asked* the waitress what she *recommended*. She *advised* the daily special, beef stew. It *was* not expensive. The service *was* slow, but the food *tasted* very good. Good cooking, they *decided*, *takes* time. They *ate* pastry for dessert and *finished* the meal with coffee.

1

10

20

30

IN GERMAN

Verbs are identified the same way as they are in English. You will find several examples of how verbs function differently in German and in English in the sections *What is an Object?*, p. 53 and *What are Reflexive Pronouns and Verbs?*, p. 141.

TERMS TO TALK ABOUT VERBS

- **Infinitive** or **dictionary form** — The verb form that is the name of the verb is called an infinitive: *to eat, to sleep, to drink*. In the dictionary a verb is listed without the "to": *eat, sleep, drink* (see *What is the Infinitive?*, p. 29).

- **Conjugation** — A verb is conjugated or changes in form to agree with its subject: *I do, he does* (see *What is a Verb Conjugation?*, p. 46).

- **Tense** — A verb indicates tense, that is, the time (present, past, or future) of the action: *I am, I was, I will be* (see *What is Meant by Tense?*, p. 102).

- **Mood** — A verb shows mood, that is, the speaker's perception that what he or she is saying is fact, command, possibility, or wish (see *What is Meant by Mood?*, p. 155).

- **Voice** — A verb shows voice, that is, the relation between the subject and the action of the verb (see *What is Meant by Active and Passive Voice?*, p. 162).

- **Participle** — A verb may be used to form a participle: *writing, written, singing, sung* (see *What is a Participle?*, p. 116).

- **Transitive** or **intransitive** — A verb can be classified as transitive or intransitive depending on whether or not the verb can take a direct object (see pp. 53-4 in *What is an Object?*).

WHAT IS AN INFINITIVE?

The **INFINITIVE** is the verb form used to name a specific verb. It is the form listed as the entry in the dictionary.

> The English-German dictionary lists *learn (v.)* **lernen**.

IN ENGLISH

In English, the infinitive is the dictionary form, that is, the one-word form found in the dictionary (*speak, dream, take)*, as well as the two-word form, *to* + the dictionary form of the verb (*to speak, to dream, to take)*. In a sentence, the infinitive is always used with the conjugated form of another verb (see *What is a Verb Conjugation?*, p. 46).

> *To study is* challenging.
> infinitive conjugated verb

> It *is* important *to be* on time.
> conjugated verb infinitive

> Axel and Gabi *want to play* tennis.
> conjugated verb infinitive

After verbs such as *must, let, should,* and *can*, English uses the dictionary form of the verb without *to*.

> Gabi *must do* her homework.
> dictionary form

> The parents *let* the children *open* the presents.
> dictionary form

IN GERMAN

As in English, the infinitive is the dictionary form. When translated into English, German infinitives are translated as *to* + verb (**arbeiten**, *to work)*. Sometimes German infinitives are preceded by **zu** (**zu arbeiten**, *to work)*. Your textbook will explain when **zu** is necessary. As in English, the infinitive is always used with the conjugated form of another verb.

The infinitive form always ends with the letters **-n** or **-en**.

*Hans wants **to play** tennis.*
Hans will Tennis **spielen.**
  conjugated verb   infinitive

40

*Ingrid doesn't have **to work.***
Ingrid braucht nicht zu **arbeiten.**
    conjugated verb   infinitive

WHAT ARE PREFIXES AND SUFFIXES?

A **PREFIX** consists of one or more syllables added to the beginning of a word to change that word's meaning.

1

nuclear	→	*anti*nuclear
approve	→	*dis*approve

A **SUFFIX** consists of one or more syllables added to the end of a word to change that word into a different part of speech.

gentle (adjective)	→	gentle*ness* (noun)
love (noun)	→	lov*able* (adjective)

To see how prefixes and suffixes work, look at the various English words that come from the Latin verb **duco** *(to lead)*. Different prefixes give us verbs such as *in*duce, *re*duce, *se*duce, pro*duce,* and intro*duce.* Added suffixes result in different parts of speech, for example: induc*tion* (noun), induc*tive* (adjective), induc*tively* (adverb).

10

IN ENGLISH

Most English prefixes and suffixes come from Latin and Greek. A good English dictionary will tell you the meaning and function of the various prefixes and suffixes.

Knowing English suffixes can help you identify the parts of speech in a sentence and increase your English vocabulary.

20

-able, -ible	toler*able*	→	adjective
-ence, -ance	reli*ance*	→	noun
-or	debt*or*	→	noun

NOUNS FORMED WITH SUFFIXES

By adding a prefix to an existing noun, you can form a new noun with a different meaning.

anti- + body (against)	→	*anti*body

30

sub- + marine (under)	→	*sub*marine

mal- + nutrition (bad)	→	*mal*nutrition

A new verb with a different meaning can be formed by adding a prefix to an existing verb.

He *used* the tool correctly.
|
verb

He *mis*used the tool, and it broke.
|
verb

A verb can also be formed by adding a prefix to another part of speech.

Anja is my new *friend*.
|
noun

She *be*friended me on my first day at the new school.
|
verb

IN GERMAN

As in English, prefixes and suffixes can be used to change the meaning of words and to change a word's part of speech.

Nouns formed with suffixes

Certain suffixes not only affect the meaning of a noun but also determine the gender of the noun being formed (see *What is Meant by Gender?*, p. 10).

- **-chen** and **-lein** → new noun is neuter
  These suffixes show that the noun is a diminutive, i.e., something reduced in size.

Noun		New noun	
das Brot	*bread*	das Brö**tchen**	*roll, little bread*
der Brief	*letter*	das Brief**lein**	*small letter*
die Frau	*woman*	das Fräu**lein**	*young woman*

- **-heit** and **-keit** → new noun is feminine
  These suffixes turn an adjective into a noun expressing an abstract quality (see *What is an Adjective?*, p. 75).

Adjective		New noun	
schön	*beautiful*	die Schön**heit**	*beauty*
frei	*free*	die Frei**heit**	*freedom*
möglich	*possible*	die Möglich**keit**	*possibility*

Verbs formed with prefixes

In the infinitive, verbs formed with a prefix are one word; i.e., the prefix is attached to the verb: ***aus*gehen** *(to go out)*, *be*suchen *(to visit).* In the other forms, verbs with prefixes are divided into two groups depending on whether or not the prefix can be separated from the verb. We shall consider each type separately.

- **Separable prefixes** — German verbs with separable prefixes are similar to English verbs that are regularly used with a preposition (see *What is a Preposition?,* p. 62); namely, they are separate words functioning as a unit with the verb.

  They *are going out* tonight at 7:00 P.M.
  |
  preposition

  He *picks up* his friend after class.
  |
  preposition

  The most common separable prefixes in German are the following: **ab-, ein-, weiter-, an-, mit-, zu-, auf-, nach-, zurück-, aus-, vor-.** Let us look at two examples to see how these prefixes can be separated from the verb.

INFINITIVE	SENTENCE
ausgehen	Hans und ich **gehen** morgen **aus.**
(to go out)	*Hans and I **are going out** tomorrow.*
ankommen	Der Zug **kommt** heute spät **an.**
(to arrive)	*The train **is arriving** late today.*

- **Inseparable prefixes** — German verbs with inseparable prefixes function as one word since these prefixes are never separated from the basic verb. The most common inseparable prefixes in German are the following: **be-, ent-, ge-, zer-, emp-, er-, ver-.** Let us look at two examples.

INFINITIVE	SENTENCE
besuchen	Wir **besuchen** unsere Tante.
(to visit)	*We **are visiting** our aunt.*
vergessen	Du **vergißt** immer dein Buch.
(to forget)	*You always **forget** your book.*

Your German textbook will explain the rules for using verbs with separable and inseparable prefixes. When you learn a new verb formed with a prefix, memorize whether the prefix is separable or not.

Flashcards

1. Create flashcards of German verbal prefixes (**an-, mit-, ver-, ent-,** etc.). On the back of the card, write "Sep" (separable) or "Insep" (inseparable). If the prefix is easily translated, add the English translation. Underneath, write an example word using that prefix.

> mit-   Sep; *with*
>   mitkommen (*to come along*)
> ver-   Insep
>   verstehen *(to understand)*

2. Create another set of flashcards. On the German side, write the infinitive of the verb stem at the top of the card. Underneath it, make two columns: one for the verb stem with separable prefixes, the other for the verb stem with inseparable prefixes. On the back, using the same layout, write the English translations.

> VERB STEM: stehen   *to stand*
>
> | SEP. PREFIX | INSEP. PREFIX | | |
> | --- | --- | --- | --- |
> | aufstehen | bestehen | *to stand up* | *to pass a test* |
> | anstehen | verstehen | *to stand in line* | *to understand* |

Practice

1. Learn the meaning of the verb stem by flipping the cards first on the German side and then on the English side (see *Tips for Learning Vocabulary*, pp. 1-3).

2. Learn the meaning of the verbs with prefixes by flipping cards as under #1. Occasionally, the meaning of the prefixes will give you a clue as to the change of meaning of the verb stem.

3. Do the above exercises orally as the verb forms with separable prefixes are pronounced differently from those with inseparable prefixes: if the prefix is separable, it is the stressed part of the verb form (**auf**stehen); if the prefix is inseparable, it is the verb stem that is the stressed part of the verb form (ver**stehen**).

WHAT IS MEANT BY CASE?

CASE in the grammatical sense means that a different form of [1]
the word is used depending on the word's function in the
sentence.

>*I* see Niko in class.
>
>| the person speaking
>function → subject

>Niko sees *me* in class.
>
>| the person speaking
>function → object
[10]

In the sentences above, the person speaking is referred to by
the forms "I" and "me." Different forms of the 1st person pronoun are used because in each sentence the person speaking
has a different grammatical function. In the first sentence, *I*
is used because the person speaking is doing the "seeing" and
in the second sentence *me* is used because the person
speaking is the object of the "seeing."

More parts of speech are affected by case in German than
in English.

ENGLISH	GERMAN	
pronouns	nouns	[20]
	pronouns	
	adjectives	
	articles	

FUNCTION OF WORDS

The grammatical role of a word in a sentence is called its
FUNCTION. The function is often based on the word's relationship to the verb (see *What is a Verb?*, p. 27). Here is a list of
the various functions a word can have, with reference to the
section in this handbook where each function is studied in [30]
detail.

- **Subject** — A noun or pronoun that performs the action of a
  verb (see *What is a Subject?*, p. 41 and *What is a Subject Pronoun?*, p. 42).
- **Predicate noun** — A noun that is linked to the subject by a
  linking verb (see *What is a Predicate Noun?*, p. 44).

■ **Object** — A noun or pronoun that is the receiver of the action of a verb (see *What is an Object?*, p. 53). There are different types of objects: direct objects (see p. 53), indirect objects (p. 55), and objects of a preposition (see p. 62).

To understand the meaning of a sentence, we must identify the function of the various words that make up the sentence. In English, the function of a word is usually indicated by where it is placed in a sentence. In German, the function of a word is established by its case form.

Knowing how to analyze the function of words in an English sentence will help you to establish which case is required in the German sentence.

IN ENGLISH

English nouns do not change form to indicate different functions (see *What is a Noun?*, p. 8). For instance, the same form of the noun is used if it is the doer of the action, (the subject) or the receiver of the action (the object). The function of a noun in a sentence is indicated by where it is placed in the sentence.

We easily recognize the difference in meaning between the following two sentences purely on the basis of word order.

> *The student* gives *the professor* the essay.
>> Here the student is giving the essay and the professor is receiving it.

> *The professor* gives *the student* the essay.
>> Here the professor is giving the essay and the student is receiving it.

These two sentences show how we can change the function of nouns by changing their place in the sentence, and consequently change the meaning of the sentence. As we shall see below, that is not the case with English pronouns.

In English the function of a personal pronoun is indicated not only by its place in the sentence, but also by its case (see *What is a Personal Pronoun?*, p. 23). As you can see in the two examples below, it is not only the word order but also the form, i.e., the case, of the pronoun that gives the sentence meaning.

> *I* know *them.*
> *They* know *me.*

We cannot say, "*I* know *they*" or "*They* know *I*" because the forms "they" and "I" can only be used to refer to the person doing the action. If you learn to recognize the different cases of pronouns in English, it will help you understand the German case system.

English pronouns have three cases.

- **Nominative case** — This case is used when a pronoun is a subject or replaces a predicate nominative (see *What is a Subject?*, p. 41 and *What is a Predicate Noun?*, p. 44).

    She and *I* went to the movies.
    └──┬──┘
    subjects
    nominative

    It was *he* who did the deed.
              │
         predicate
         nominative

- **Objective case** — This case is used when a pronoun is an object (see *What is an Object?*, p. 53).

    They saw *him*.
     │   │
    subject object
    nominative objective

    He sent *them* a note.
     │   │
    subject object
    nominative objective

- **Possessive case** — This case is used when a pronoun shows ownership (see *What is a Possessive Pronoun?*, p. 81).

    Is this book *yours*?
                    │
              possessive

    Julia called her parents, but I wrote *mine* an e-mail.
                                             │
                                        possessive

IN GERMAN

Unlike English where only pronouns change form to indicate case, in German many parts of speech change form depending on the function of the word in the sentence. The case of a German word is sometimes reflected not only by a particular form of the word itself, but also by the form of the words that accompany it. We have limited the examples in this section to the case of nouns and their accompanying articles (see *What is a Noun?*, p. 8 and *What is an Article?*, p. 17).

German has four different cases, and each case reflects a different function of the word in a sentence.

- **Nominative case** — This case is used for the subject of a sentence and for predicate nouns (see *What is a Subject?*, p. 41 and *What is a Predicate Noun?*, p. 44). This is the form of nouns listed in a vocabulary list or a dictionary.

- **Accusative case** — This case is used for most direct objects and after certain prepositions (see *What is an Object?*, p. 53 and *What is a Preposition?*, p. 62).

- **Dative case** — This case is used primarily for indirect objects and after certain prepositions.

- **Genitive case** — This case is used to show possession or close relation, and after certain prepositions (see *What is the Possessive?*, p. 86).

The case of a noun can be indicated by the form of the noun itself, usually in its ending, as well as by the ending of the accompanying article. Each case has a singular and plural form (see *What is Meant by Number?*, p. 14). The complete set of case forms for any noun is called the noun's DECLENSION. When you have memorized these forms, you are able to "decline" that noun.

Case affects the form of masculine and neuter nouns in the genitive singular and of all nouns in the dative plural.

- masculine and neuter nouns, genitive singular → add –(e)s

SINGULAR

NOMINATIVE	GENITIVE
Mann (m. sing.)	Mann**es**
Kind (neut. sing.)	Kind**es**

- all nouns, dative plural → add –**n** (if they don't already end with –**n**)

PLURAL

NOMINATIVE	DATIVE
Männer (m. sing.)	Männer**n**
Kinder (neut. sing.)	Kinder**n**
Frauen (f. sing.)	Frauen

Refer to your textbook for a small group of nouns called WEAK NOUNS or N-NOUNS that do not follow the pattern above and have different endings to indicate case.

When case is not indicated by the form of the noun itself, it is the definite or indefinite article that accompanies the noun that reflects the number, gender, and function of the noun.

- masculine singular articles → four case forms

	DEF.	INDEF.
NOM.	der	ein
ACC.	den	einen
DAT.	dem	einem
GEN.	des	eines

170

- feminine singular articles → two case forms

	DEF.	INDEF.
NOM. & ACC.	die	eine
DAT. & GEN.	der	einer

- neuter singular articles → three case forms

	DEF.	INDEF.
NOM. & ACC.	das	ein
DAT.	dem	einem
GEN.	des	eines

180

- plural of all articles → three case forms

	DEF.	INDEF.
NOM. & ACC.	die	keine
DAT.	den	keinen
GEN.	der	keiner

Below is a chart illustrating how nouns and their accompanying article work hand in hand to indicate case: in the singular, a masculine noun **der Mann** *(man)*, a feminine noun **die Frau** *(woman)*, and a neuter noun **das Kind** *(child)*, and in the plural **die Kinder** *(children)* that serves all genders.

190

	SINGULAR			PLURAL
	MASCULINE	FEMININE	NEUTER	
NOMINATIVE	**der** Mann	**die** Frau	**das** Kind	**die** Kinder
ACCUSATIVE	**den** Mann	**die** Frau	**das** Kind	**die** Kinder
DATIVE	**dem** Mann	**der** Frau	**dem** Kind	**den** Kindern
GENITIVE	**des** Mannes	**der** Frau	**des** Kindes	**der** Kinder

200

When the nouns are in their proper case, words in the sentence can be moved around without changing the essential meaning of the sentence. Look at the many ways one sentence can be expressed in German.

The mother gives *the* child *the* apple.
Die Mutter gibt **dem** Kind **den** Apfel.

nominative   dative   accusative
the mother   gives   the child   the apple

Den Apfel gibt **die** Mutter **dem** Kind.
Dem Kind gibt **die** Mutter **den** Apfel.

To choose the appropriate case for each noun in the German sentences above, you need to go through a series of steps:

1. GENDER — Identify the gender and number of each noun in the sentence.
    mother → **die Mutter**→ feminine singular
    child → **das Kind** → neuter singular
    apple → **der Apfel** → masculine singular

2. FUNCTION — Determine how each noun functions in the sentence.
    mother → subject
    child → indirect object
    apple → direct object

3. CASE — Determine what case in German corresponds to the function identified in step two.
    mother → subject →* nominative case
    child → indirect object →* dative case
    apple → direct object →* accusative case

4. SELECTION — Choose the proper form from the declension you have memorized.

Die Mutter gibt dem Kind den Apfel.

feminine   neuter   masculine
singular   singular   singular
nominative   dative   accusative

Your textbook will show you the different case forms for the definite and indefinite articles and explain how to use them. As you learn more German, you will discover other ways in which case affects the form of nouns, pronouns, and adjectives (see *What is an Adjective?*, p. 75).

What is an Adjective?, p. 75

STUDY TIPS

Flashcards
Using the chart on p. 39, make cards illustrating each case by writing the German noun and accompanying article on one side; on the other side, indicate the gender, case, and number of the noun.

dem Kind	neuter, dative, singular
einer Frau	feminine, dative or genitive, singular
die Kinder	neuter, nominative or accusative, plural

WHAT IS A SUBJECT?

In a sentence the person or thing that performs the action of
the verb is called the **SUBJECT**.

> *The teacher* corrected the tests.
>
>   subject   verb

IN ENGLISH

To find the subject of a sentence, always look for the verb
first; then ask, *who?* or *what?* before the verb (see *What is a
Verb?*, p. 27). The answer will be the subject.

> Lukas studies German.
> VERB: studies
> *Who* studies German? ANSWER: Lukas → subject
> The subject is singular (see p. 14). It refers to one person.

> Did the packages come yesterday?
> VERB: come
> *What* came yesterday? ANSWER: packages → subject
> The subject is plural. It refers to more than one thing.

If a sentence has more than one verb, you have to find the
subject of each verb.

> The boys were cooking while Ingrid set the table.
> *Boys* is the subject of *were*.
> Note that the subject is plural.
>
> *Ingrid* is the subject of *set*.
> Note that the subject is singular.

IN GERMAN

In German, it is important that you recognize the subject
of a sentence so that you can put it in the proper case (see
What is Meant by Case?, p. 35). The subject of a German
sentence is in the nominative case.

> **Das Kind** spielt allein.
> *The child plays alone.*
> *Who* plays? ANSWER: the child
> *Child* (**das Kind**) is the subject, therefore **das Kind** is in the
> nominative case.

CAREFUL — In English and in German it is important to find
the subject of each verb so that you can choose the form of
the verb that goes with that subject (see *What is a Verb Conjugation?*, p. 46).

CHAPTER

WHAT IS A SUBJECT PRONOUN?

Pronouns used as subjects are called **SUBJECT PRONOUNS** (see *What is a Subject?*, p. 41).

> *They* ran, but *I* walked.
> Who ran? ANSWER: They.
> *They* is the subject of the verb *ran*.
>
> Who walked? ANSWER: I.
> *I* is the subject of the verb *walked*.

IN ENGLISH

Below is a list of English subject pronouns. For an explanation of the various "persons" see p. 23.

SINGULAR

1ST PERSON	I
2ND PERSON	you
3RD PERSON	he, she, it

PLURAL

1ST PERSON	we
2ND PERSON	you
3RD PERSON	they

The above personal pronouns can only be used as subjects of the verb. English uses another set of pronouns when the pronoun is an object of the verb (see *What are Direct and Indirect Object Pronouns?*, p. 57 and *What is an Object of Preposition Pronoun?*, p. 67).

IN GERMAN

The **NOMINATIVE CASE** of the pronoun is used as subject of the verb (see *What is a Verb?*, p. 27 and p. 38 in *What is Meant by Case?*).

	ENGLISH	GERMAN NOMINATIVE	
SINGULAR			
1ST PERSON	*I*	ich	
2ND PERSON	*you*	du	FAMILIAR
		Sie	FORMAL
3RD PERSON	*he*	er	MASCULINE
	she	sie	FEMININE
	it	er	MASCULINE
		sie	FEMININE
		es	NEUTER

PLURAL

1ST PERSON	*we*	wir	
2ND PERSON	*you*	ihr	FAMILIAR
		Sie	FORMAL
3RD PERSON	*they*	sie	

40

To help you select the proper German subject pronoun, see pp. 23-6 in *What is a Personal Pronoun?*.

CHAPTER

14

WHAT IS A PREDICATE NOUN?

A **PREDICATE NOUN** is a noun connected to the subject by a linking verb. A **LINKING VERB** is a verb that acts as an equal sign linking interchangeable elements.

> Johan is my friend. [Johan = friend]
> subject | predicate noun
> linking verb

IN ENGLISH

The most common linking verbs are *to be* and *to become*. The noun that follows the linking verb is not an object because it does not receive the action of the verb (see *What is an Object?*, p. 53); instead, it is a predicate noun because it is interchangeable with the subject.

> Ingrid *is* a good student.
> linking verb   predicate noun

> LINKING VERB: *is* (form of *to be*)
> SUBJECT: *Ingrid*
> PREDICATE NOUN: *student (Ingrid = student)*

> Axel became a teacher.
> linking verb   predicate noun

> LINKING VERB: *became* (form of *to become*)
> SUBJECT: *Axel*
> PREDICATE NOUN: *teacher (Axel = teacher)*

IN GERMAN

The most common linking verbs are **sein** *(to be)*, **werden** *(to become)* and **scheinen** *(to appear)*. As in English, the noun following a linking verb is a predicate noun, not an object. Predicate nouns are in the nominative case, the same case as the subject (see *What is Meant by Case?*, p. 35).

> Gabi ist meine **Freundin**.
> nom. linking   nom.
> case verb   case

> LINKING VERB: **ist** (form of **sein** *to be*)
> SUBJECT = PREDICATE NOUN: **Gabi** = **Freundin** *(friend)*
> Both **Gabi** and **Freundin** are in the nominative case.

*Gabi is my **friend**.*

Axel wurde **Lehrer**.

nom.	linking	nom.
case	verb	case

> LINKING VERB: **wurde** (form of **werden** *to become*) [40]
> SUBJECT = PREDICATE NOUN: **Axel** = **Lehrer** *(teacher)*
> Both **Axel** and **Lehrer** are in the nominative case.

*Axel became a **teacher**.*

CAREFUL — It is important that you distinguish predicate nouns from objects so that you can put them in the nominative case.

STUDY TIPS — PREDICATE NOUNS

Flashcards
On the English side of your cards for the verbs **sein, werden**, and **scheinen** indicate "linking verb, predicate noun takes nominative case", with an example.

> Herr Meier ist der Lehrer.
> N   N

CHAPTER

15

WHAT IS A VERB CONJUGATION?

1   A **VERB CONJUGATION** is a list of the six possible forms of the verb for a particular tense (see *What is Meant by Tense?*, p. 102). For each tense, there is one verb form for each of the six persons used as the subject of the verb (see *What is a Subject?*, p. 41).

> I am
> you are
> he, she, it is
> we are
> you are
> they are

10 Different tenses have different verb forms, but the principle of conjugation remains the same. In this chapter all our examples are in the present tense (see *What is the Present Tense?*, p. 104).

IN ENGLISH

The verb *to be* conjugated above is the English verb that changes the most; it has three forms: *am, are,* and *is.* (In conversation the initial vowel is often replaced by an apostrophe: *I'm, you're, he's*). Other English verbs only have two forms. Let us look at the verb *to sing.*

20 **SINGULAR**

1ST PERSON		I sing
2ND PERSON		you sing
3RD PERSON	{	he sings
		she sings
		it sings

PLURAL

1ST PERSON	we sing
2ND PERSON	you sing
3RD PERSON	they sing

30 Because English verbs change so little, it isn't necessary to learn "to conjugate a verb;" that is, to list all its possible forms. For most verbs, it is much simpler to say that the verb adds an "(e)-s" in the 3rd person singular.

IN GERMAN

Unlike English, German verb forms change from one person to another so that when you learn a new verb you must also learn how to conjugate it. The conjugation of all regular and many irregular verbs, however, does follow a predictable pattern.

In the conjugation of most regular and irregular German verbs, there are four forms that look like the infinitive of the verb: the 1st and 3rd persons plural and the 2nd person formal, singular and plural (see *What is the Infinitive?* p. 29).

CHOOSING THE CORRECT "PERSON" (see p. 24)

In your textbook, the 2nd person formal forms will either be listed after the 2nd person familiar plural forms or after the 3rd person plural form, as they are in the conjugation of the verb **singen** *(to sing)* below.

SINGULAR

1ST PERSON	ich singe	*I sing*
2ND PERSON FAMILIAR	du singst	*you sing*
3RD PERSON	er singt sie singt es singt	*he, it sings* *she, it sings* *it sings*

PLURAL

1ST PERSON	wir singen	*we sing*
2ND PERSON FAMILIAR	ihr singt	*you sing*
3RD PERSON	sie singen	*they sing*
2ND PERSON FORMAL (sing. & pl.)	Sie singen	*you sing*

To choose the proper verb form, it is important to identify the person and the number of the subject.

1st person singular — The subject is always **ich** *(I)*.

> **Ich** singe leise.
> *I sing softly.*

Notice that **ich** is not capitalized, except when it is the first word of a sentence.

2nd person singular familiar — The subject is always **du** *(you)*.

> Katrin, **du** singst gut.
> *Katrin, **you** sing well.*

3rd person singular — The subject can be expressed in one of three ways:

- the 3rd person singular masculine pronoun **er** *(he or it)*, the feminine pronoun **sie** *(she or it)*, and the neuter pronoun **es** *(it)*

Er singt schön.
He sings beautifully.

Sie singt schön.
She sings beautifully.

Es singt schön.
It sings beautifully.

- a proper noun

    Anna singt gut.
    Anna sings well.

    Der Fischer Chor singt gut.
    The Fischer choir sings well.

    Since the proper noun could be replaced by the pronoun *he, she* or *it* (**er**, **sie**, or **es**), you must use the 3rd person singular form of the verb.

- a singular common noun

    Der Vogel singt.
    The bird sings.

    Die Geige singt.
    The violin sings.

    Das Kind singt.
    The child sings.

    Since the common noun could be replaced by the pronoun *he, she* or *it* (**er**, **sie**, or **es**), you must use the 3rd person singular form of the verb.

1st person plural — The subject can be expressed in one of two ways:

- the 1st person plural pronoun **wir** *(we)*

    Wir singen gut.
    We sing well.

- a multiple subject in which the speaker is included

    Axel, Lukas, Ingrid und ich singen gut.
    Axel, Lukas, Ingrid and I sing well.

    Since the subject could be replaced by the pronoun *we* (**wir**), you must use the 1st person plural form of the verb.

2nd person plural familiar — The subject is always **ihr** *(you).*

Ingrid und Lukas, singt **ihr** auch?
*Ingrid and Lukas, do **you** sing too?*

Since the subjects *Ingrid* and *Lukas* (whom you would address with the 2nd person familiar individually), could be replaced by the pronoun *you* (**ihr**), you must use the 2nd person plural familiar form of the verb.

2nd person formal (singular and plural) — The subject is always **Sie** *(you)*.

Frau Meier, kommen **Sie** mit?
*Mrs. Meier, are **you** coming along with us?*

Herr und Frau Meier, kommen **Sie** mit?
*Mr. and Mrs. Meier, are **you** coming along with us?*

> Since the subjects *Mr.* and *Mrs. Meier* (whom you would address with the 2nd person formal individually or together) could be replaced by the pronoun *you* (**Sie**), you must use the 2nd person formal form of the verb.

130

3rd person plural — The subject can be expressed in one of three ways:

- the 3rd person plural pronoun **sie** *(they)*

Sie singen im Chor.
They sing in the choir.

- a plural noun

Die Kinder singen im Chor.
The children sing in the choir.

140

> Since the plural noun could be replaced by the 3rd person plural pronoun *they* (**sie**), you must use the 3rd person plural form of the verb.

- two or more proper or common nouns

Lukas und Ingrid singen ein Duett.
Lukas and Ingrid sing a duet.

Die Gläser und Teller sind auf dem Tisch.
The glasses and plates are on the table.

> Since the nouns could be replaced by the 3rd person plural pronoun *they* (**sie**), you must use the 3rd person plural form of the verb.

150

HOW TO CONJUGATE A VERB

A German verb is composed of two parts, a stem and an ending.

- **The stem** — the part of the verb left after dropping the final **-en** from the infinitive (or with a few verbs like **tun** and **ändern** by dropping the final **-n**).

INFINITIVE	STEM
singen	sing-
machen	mach-
kommen	komm-

160

In regular verbs the stem remains the same throughout a conjugation in the present tense. However, in certain verbs called **STEM-CHANGING VERBS**, the stem vowel changes in 2nd and 3rd person singular (**geben** → **du gibst**; **lesen** → **du liest**; **fahren** → **du fährst**). Your textbook will identify which verbs are stem-changing verbs.

- **The ending** — the part of the verb that is added to the stem and that corresponds to the grammatical person.

As an example of the steps to follow to conjugate a verb, let us look at the regular verb **machen** *(to make)*.

1. Find the verb stem by removing the infinitive ending.

   INFINITIVE: **machen** → STEM: **mach-**

2. Add the ending that agrees with the subject.

SINGULAR

1ST PERSON	ich mache	*I make*
2ND PERSON FAMILIAR	du machst	*you make*
	er macht	*he, it makes*
3RD PERSON	sie macht	*she, it makes*
	es macht	*it makes*

PLURAL

1ST PERSON	wir machen	*we make*
2ND PERSON FAMILIAR	ihr macht	*you make*
3RD PERSON	sie machen	*they make*
2ND PERSON FORMAL (sing. & pl.)	Sie machen	*you make*

As irregular verbs are introduced in your textbook, either their entire conjugation or their principal parts will be given so that you will know how to conjugate them (see *What are the Principal Parts of a Verb?*, p. 109). Be sure to memorize these forms, because many common verbs are irregular (**sein**, *to be;* **gehen**, *to go;* **werden**, *to become,* for example).

STUDY TIPS — VERB CONJUGATIONS

Pattern (see *Tips for Learning Word Forms*, p. 3)

1. Start by looking for a pattern within the conjugation of the verb itself. For example, let's find a pattern in the regular verbs **wohnen** *(to live)* and **machen** *(to make)* above.

ich wohne	wir wohnen
du wohnst	ihr wohnt
er/sie/es wohnt	sie wohnen/Sie Wohnen

What pattern do you see?

- all the forms start with the same stem: **wohn-** and **mach-**
- **ich** forms have an -e ending
- **du** forms have an -st ending
- **er/sie/es** and **ihr** have a -t ending
- **wir, sie** (pl.) and **Sie** have an **-en** ending

2. Whenever you learn a new verb, look for similarities with another verb.

The pattern can be related to the consonant ending the stem. For example, let's look at fin**d**en *(to find)*, arbei**t**en *(to work)* and öff**n**en *(to open)*.

ich finde	wir finden	ich arbeite	wir arbeiten	ich öffne	wir öffnen
du findest	ihr findet	du arbeitest	ihr arbeitet	du öffnest	ihr öffnet
er.. findet	sie/Sie finden	er.. arbeitet	sie/Sie arbeiten	er.. öffnet	sie/Sie öffnen

What similarities and differences with regular verbs (see under 1 above) do you see?

- the endings of the verb forms are the same, except for **du, er/sie/es** and **ihr** that insert an -e before the ending

The pattern can be related to the vowel of the stem. For example, let's look at three stem-changing verbs st**e**hen *(to see)*, schl**a**fen *(to sleep)* and g**e**ben *(to give)*.

ich sehe	wir sehen	ich schlafe	wir schlafen	ich gebe	wir geben
du siehst	ihr seht	du schläfst	ihr schlaft	du gibst	ihr gebt
er.. sieht	sie/Sie sehen	er.. schläft	sie/Sie schlafen	er.. gibt	sie/Sie geben

What similarities and differences with regular verbs (see under 1 above) do you see?

- the endings of all the verb forms are the same
- the stem vowel changes only in the **du** and **er/sie/es** forms
- vowels change in the same way in the **du** and **er/sie/es** forms

3. As new verb conjugations are introduced, more and more similarities and patterns will become evident. Take the time to look for them.

Flashcards

Create a card for each verb to memorize its meaning and conjugation pattern. On the German side, write the infinitive form and the following information as appropriate:

1. If it is a stem-changing verb, indicate its type (**a → ä; e → i; e → ie**) in parentheses.

fahren (a → ä)	*to drive*
geben (e → i)	*to give*
lesen (e → ie)	*to read*

2. If the verb requires a spelling change in the **du** or **er/sie/es** endings due to particular consonant combinations, write the form in parentheses and underline the spelling change.

reden (er red**e**t)	*to talk*
arbeiten (er arbei**te**t)	*to work*
tanzen (du tan**z**t)	*to dance*

Practice

1. Learn the different forms of a verb by writing them down (always using the subject pronoun). Repeat until you can write the correct forms without referring to your textbook.

2. Practice using the various forms out of order, so that if you are asked a question you can respond without going through the entire pattern.

3. Be sure to do the exercises that follow the introduction of a new con-jugation. When you've finished, refer to your textbook or answer key to make corrections. Mark the mistakes and corrections with a col-ored pen so that they stand out and you can concentrate on them when you review.

4. Write your own sentences using the different forms of the verb.

See also *Study Tips — Principal Parts of Verbs* (p. 111).

WHAT IS AN OBJECT?

An **OBJECT** is a noun or pronoun that is connected to the
action of the verb or to a preposition.

Niko *writes* a letter.

    verb   direct
             object

Niko *writes* his mother.

      verb   indirect
              object

The boy left *with* his father.

       preposition object of a
                  preposition

In this chapter we will study the direct object and the indirect
object. The object of a preposition is covered in *What is a Preposition?*, p. 62. Although we have limited the examples in this
section to noun objects, the same procedure can be used to
establish the function of pronoun objects.

DIRECT OBJECT

(see also *What are Direct and Indirect Object Pronouns?*, p. 57)

IN ENGLISH

A direct object is a noun or pronoun that receives the
action of the verb directly, without a preposition between
the verb and the noun or pronoun. It answers the question *whom?* or *what?* asked after the verb.

Axel sees *Ingrid.*
    Axel sees *whom?* Ingrid.
    Ingrid is the direct object.

Axel writes *a letter.*
    Axel writes *what?* A letter.
    A letter is the direct object.

There are two types of verbs: transitive and intransitive.

- **transitive verb** — a verb that takes a direct object. It is
  indicated by the abbreviation *v.t.* (verb transitive) in dictionaries.

    The boy *threw* the ball.

     transitive   direct object

She *lost* her job.
      | |
transitive direct object

- **intransitive verb** — a verb that cannot take a direct object. It is indicated by the abbreviation *v.i.* (verb intransitive) in dictionaries.

Ingrid *arrives* today.
    | |
intransitive adverb

Franz *is sleeping*.
    |_____|
intransitive

Many verbs can be used both transitively, that is, with a direct object, and intransitively, without a direct object.

The students *speak* German.
       | |
transitive direct object

Actions *speak* louder than words.
    | |_____|
intransitive adverbial phrase

CAREFUL — Some verbs that are transitive in English are intransitive in German, while other verbs that are intransitive in English are transitive in German.

IN GERMAN

As in English, a direct object is a noun or pronoun that receives the action of the verb directly. It answers the question **wen?** *(whom?)* or **was?** *(what?)* asked after the verb. Direct objects are expressed by the accusative case in German.

Niko liest **das Buch**.
    Niko reads *what?* The book.
    Das Buch is the direct object → accusative case
    *Niko reads **the book**.*

A few verbs take dative case objects in German instead of accusative case objects. Here are two examples.

- **danken** *(to thank)*
    Sie danken **dem Polizisten**.
        They thank *whom?* The policeman (**dem Polizisten**).
        Dem Polizisten is the direct object, but in the dative case.
        *They thank **the policeman**.*

- **helfen** *(to help)*
    Wir helfen **dir**.
        We are helping *whom?* You (**dir**).
        Dir is the direct object, but in the dative case.
        *We are helping **you**.*

Your German textbook will indicate the verbs that take objects in the dative case, and you will need to memorize them.   80

CAREFUL — An English verb that requires a preposition before its object (see *What is a Preposition?*, p. 62) may have an equivalent German verb that requires a direct object in the accusative.

> *She is looking for **her coat**.*
>> She is looking *for what? Her coat* is the object of the preposition *for*.
>
> Sie sucht **ihren Mantel**.   90
>> |
>
> **suchen** *(to look for)* takes a direct object → accusative case

INDIRECT OBJECT
(see also *What are Direct and Indirect Object Pronouns?*, p. 57)

IN ENGLISH
An indirect object is a noun or pronoun that receives the action of the verb indirectly. It answers the question *to* or *for whom?* or *to* or *for what?* asked after the verb.

> Axel wrote *his brother*.
>> He wrote *to whom?* His brother.   100
>> *His brother* is the indirect object.
>
> Axel did *his brother* a favor.
>> He did a favor *for whom?* His brother.
>> *His brother* is the indirect object.

Sometimes the word *to* is included in the English sentence.

> Axel spoke *to Lukas and Ingrid*.
>> Axel spoke *to whom?* To Lukas and Ingrid.
>> *Lukas* and *Ingrid* are two indirect objects.

IN GERMAN   110
As in English, an indirect object is a noun or pronoun that receives the action of the verb indirectly. It answers the question **wem?** *(to* or *for whom?)* or **was?** *(to* or *for what?)* asked after the verb. Indirect objects are expressed by the dative case in German.

> Niko schreibt **seinem Bruder**.
>> Niko writes *to whom?* His brother.
>> **Seinem Bruder** is the indirect object → dative case
> *Niko writes **(to) his brother**.*
>
> Ingrid tat **mir** einen Gefallen.   120
>> Ingrid did a favor *for whom?* Me.
>> **Mir** is the indirect object → dative case
> *Ingrid did **me** a favor.*

SENTENCES WITH A DIRECT AND AN INDIRECT OBJECT

A sentence may contain both a direct object and an indirect object, either as nouns or pronouns.

IN ENGLISH

When a sentence has both a direct and an indirect object, two word orders are possible, one without "to" preceding the indirect object and one with the preposition "to".

- If the indirect object is not preceded by "to," the word order is as follows: subject (S) + verb (V) + indirect object (IO) + direct object (DO).

      Johan gave his sister a gift.
       | | | |
       S   V   IO   DO

      Who gave a gift? Johan.
      Johan is the subject.

      Johan gave *what?* A gift.
      A gift is the direct object.

      Johan gave a gift *to whom?* His sister.
      His sister is the indirect object.

- If the indirect object is preceded by "to," the word order is as follows: subject + verb + direct object + *to* + indirect object.

      Johan gave a gift to his sister.
       | | | |
       S   V   DO   IO

The first structure without "to" is the most common. However, since there is no "to" preceding the indirect object *(sister),* it is more difficult to identify its function than in the second structure.

IN GERMAN

As in English, a sentence can have both a direct and an indirect object. The order of the objects in the German sentence depends on whether they are nouns or pronouns and on their function. For example:

 nouns → indirect object + direct object

- pronouns → direct object + indirect object
- pronoun and noun → pronoun + noun

Consult your textbook.

17

WHAT ARE DIRECT AND INDIRECT OBJECT PRONOUNS?

Pronouns used as direct and indirect objects are called **OBJECT**   1
PRONOUNS.

> Michael saw *us.*
>> Michael saw *whom?* Us.
>>> *Us* is the direct object of *saw.*
>
> My parents wrote *me.*
>> My parents wrote *to whom?* Me.
>>> *Me* is the indirect object of *wrote.*

The various functions of object pronouns are established in
the same way as the function of object nouns (see *What is an*   10
Object?, p. 53).

IN ENGLISH

Pronouns used as direct and indirect objects in English are
different in form from the ones used as subjects.

	SUBJECT	**OBJECT**
SINGULAR		
1ST PERSON	I	me
2ND PERSON	you	you
3RD PERSON	he	him
	she	her
	it	it
PLURAL		
1ST PERSON	we	us
2ND PERSON	you	you
3RD PERSON	they	them

Here are a few examples of the usage of nominative and
objective pronouns.

> *He* and *I* work for the newspaper.
>> subjects: 3rd pers. sing. + 1st pers. sing.   30
>> nominative case
>
> The politician invited *him* and *me* to lunch.
>> direct objects: 3rd pers. sing. + 1st pers. sing.
>> objective case

They took their car to the garage.

subject: 3rd pers. pl.
nominative case

I lent *them* my car.

indirect object: 3rd pers. pl.
objective case

IN GERMAN

Unlike English that has only one objective case for pronouns, German uses two cases, the accusative and the dative. Look at the chart below.

ENGLISH OBJECTIVE		GERMAN		
		ACCUSATIVE	DATIVE	
SINGULAR 1ST PERSON	*me*	mich	mir	
2ND PERSON	*you*	dich Sie	dir Ihnen	FAMILIAR FORMAL
3RD PERSON	*him* *her* *it*	ihn sie es	ihm ihr ihm	MASCULINE FEMININE NEUTER
PLURAL 1ST PERSON	*us*	uns	uns	
2ND PERSON	*you*	euch Sie	euch Ihnen	FAMILIAR FORMAL
3RD PERSON	*them*	sie	ihnen	

Two English object pronouns have more than one equivalent in German: *you* and *it*. Let us look more closely at these two object pronouns.

FAMILIAR "YOU" AS OBJECT PRONOUN

(see pp. 24-5 in *What is a Personal Pronoun?*)

The familiar forms of "you" can be singular or plural, depending on whether the "you" addressed is one or more persons, each form having an accusative and dative form.

■ **singular** — You are speaking to one person → **dich** (accusative); **dir** (dative)

> *We see **you**, Anna.*
> Wir sehen **dich**, Anna.

sehen *(to see)* takes an accusative object

*We are helping **you**, Anna.*
Wir helfen **dir**, Anna.

helfen *(to help)* takes a dative object

- **plural** — You are speaking to more than one person → **euch** (accusative and dative)

80

  *We see **you**, Effi and Franz.*
  Wir sehen **euch**, Effi und Franz.

  sehen *(to see)* takes an accusative object

  *We are helping **you**, Effi and Franz.*
  Wir helfen **euch**, Effi und Franz.

  helfen *(to help)* takes a dative object

FORMAL "YOU" AS OBJECT PRONOUN
(see pp. 24-5 in *What is a Personal Pronoun?*)

The formal form of "you" has two forms, the accusative and the dative; the same form is used for the singular and the plural.

90

- **accusative** — You are speaking to one or more persons → **Sie** (accusative singular and plural)

  *We will see **you** tomorrow, Mrs. Erb.*
  Wir sehen **Sie** morgen, Frau Erb.

  sehen *(to see)* takes an accusative object

- **dative** — You are speaking to one or more persons → **Ihnen** (dative singular and plural)

100

  *We are glad to help **you**, Dr. Fried.*
  Wir helfen **Ihnen** gern, Dr. Fried.

  helfen *(to help)* takes a dative object

"IT" AS OBJECT PRONOUN

Like English, German uses personal pronouns in the objective case to refer to people, **ihn**, **ihm** *(him)* and **sie**, **ihr** *(her)*. But where English uses one pronoun for "it," German has six different object pronouns depending on the gender of the antecedent and the case of the pronoun, accusative or dative.

110

To choose the correct form, follow these steps:

1. ANTECEDENT: Find the noun "it" replaces.
2. GENDER: Determine the gender of the German antecedent.
3. FUNCTION: Determine the function of "it" in the sentence.
4. CASE: Choose the case that corresponds to the function.
5. SELECTION: Select the form depending on the gender (step 2) and case (step 4).

Let us look at some examples.

- masculine antecedent → **ihn** (accusative) or **ihm** (dative)

  Did you see the film? Yes, I saw it.

  ANTECEDENT: the film
  GENDER: **der Film** *(the film)* → masculine
  FUNCTION: direct object of *see* (**sehen**)
  CASE: accusative
  SELECTION: masculine accusative → **ihn**

  Hast du den Film gesehen? Ja, ich habe **ihn** gesehen.

- feminine antecedent → **sie** (accusative) or **ihr** (dative)

  Are you reading the newspaper? Yes, I am reading it.

  ANTECEDENT: the newspaper
  GENDER: **die Zeitung** *(the newspaper)* → feminine
  FUNCTION: direct object of *read* (**lesen**)
  CASE: accusative
  SELECTION: feminine accusative → **sie**

  Lesen Sie die Zeitung? Ja, ich lese **sie**.

- neuter antecedent → **es** (accusative) or **ihm** (dative)

  Do you understand the book? Yes, I understand it.

  ANTECEDENT: the book
  GENDER: **das Buch** *(the book)* → neuter
  FUNCTION: direct object of *understand* (**verstehen**)
  CASE: accusative
  SELECTION: neuter accusative → **es**

  Verstehen Sie das Buch? Ja, ich verstehe **es**.

CAREFUL — In English you can only use the objective pronouns *him* or *her* to refer to people. In German, however, when you replace neuter nouns that refer to people you have to use the neuter pronouns **es** and **ihm**.

  Who helps the child? We are helping her (or him).

  ANTECEDENT: the child
  GENDER: **das Kind** *(the child)* → neuter
  FUNCTION: object of *help* (**helfen** takes a dative object)
  CASE: dative
  SELECTION: neuter dative → **ihm**

  Wer hilft dem Kind? Wir helfen **ihm**.
  dative object

Flashcard

On the personal pronoun flashcards (see p. 26), add sentences illustrating the pronoun's direct and indirect object forms. Underline the object pronouns; this will draw your attention to form changes depending on the pronoun's function in the sentence.

er	*he, it* (subject)
Ich sehe <u>ihn</u>.	*I see him/it.* (direct object)
Ich gebe <u>ihm</u> das Buch.	*I give him the book.* (indirect object)
sie	*they* (subject)
Ich sehe <u>sie</u>.	*I see them.* (direct object)
Ich gebe <u>ihnen</u> das Buch.	*I give them the book.* (indirect object)

Pattern

1. Look for similarities between direct object pronouns (accusative) and other parts of speech. Refer to the chart on p. 58.

   What pattern do you see?
   - 1st and 2nd pers. sing. (**mich, dich**) the same initial letters (**m-, d-**) as possessive adjectives (**mein, dein**), chart p. 84
   - 2nd pers. formal (**Sie**) and 3rd pers. pl. (**sie**) same as subject pronoun, chart pp. 42-3
   - 3rd pers. sing. and pl. pronoun (**-n, -e, -s; e**) the same last letter as definite articles for direct objects (**den, die, das; die**), chart p. 39

2. Look for similarities between direct object pronouns (accusative) and indirect object pronouns (dative), as well as other parts of speech.

   What pattern do you see?
   - 1st and 2nd pers. informal sing. (**mir, dir**): direct object ending **–ch** (**mich, dich**) changes to **–r** in indirect object
   - 1st and 2nd pers. informal pl. (**uns, euch**): same forms for direct and indirect object pronouns
   - 2nd pers. formal (**Sie, Sie, Ihnen**) and 3rd pers. plural (**sie, sie, ihnen**): same forms for subject, direct, and indirect pronouns, except for capitalization.
   - 3rd pers. sing. and pl. indirect object pronoun last letter (**-m, -r, -m; n**): same as definite articles for indirect objects (**dem, der, dem; den**)

Practice

1. Write a series of short German sentences with masculine, feminine, neuter, and plural direct objects. Rewrite the sentences replacing the direct object with the appropriate object pronoun.

Ich kaufe die Blumen.	*I buy the flowers.*
Ich kaufe sie.	*I buy them.*

2. Add an indirect object to the original sentences you created under 1 above. Rewrite the sentences replacing the indirect object with the appropriate object pronoun.

Ich kaufe meiner Mutter die Blumen.	*I buy my mom flowers.*
Ich kaufe ihr die Blumen.	*I buy her flowers.*

3. Replace both the direct and indirect objects with pronouns in the sentences you've created under 2. Refer to your textbook for the correct word order.

Ich kaufe sie ihr.	*I buy them for her.*

CHAPTER

WHAT IS A PREPOSITION?

A **PREPOSITION** is a word that shows the relationship of one word (usually a noun or pronoun) to another word (usually another noun or pronoun) in the sentence. The noun or pronoun following the preposition is called the **OBJECT OF THE PREPOSITION**. The preposition plus its object is called a **PREPOSITIONAL PHRASE**.

prepositional phrase

Paul has an appointment *after* school.

preposition   object of preposition

IN ENGLISH

Prepositions normally indicate location, direction, time, or manner.

- prepositions showing location or position

    Michael was *in* the car.
    Anna is sitting *behind* you.

- prepositions showing direction

    We went *to* school.
    The students came directly *from* class.

- prepositions showing time and date

    Many Germans vacation *in* August.
    Their son will be home *at* Christmas.
    I'm meeting him *before* 4:30 today.

- prepositions showing manner

    He writes *with* a pen.
    They left *without* us.

Other frequently used prepositions are: *during, since, between, of, about.* Some English prepositions are made up of more than a single word: *because of, in front of, instead of, due to, in spite of, on account of.*

An object of a preposition is a noun or pronoun that follows a preposition and is related to it. It answers the question *whom?* or *what?* asked after the preposition.

Franz is leaving without Effi.

Franz is leaving *without whom?* Without Effi.

Effi is the noun object of the preposition *without.*

The baby eats with a spoon.

> The baby eats *with what?* With a spoon.
>
> *A spoon* is the noun object of the preposition *with.*

Johan goes out with her.

> Johan goes out *with whom?* With her.
>
> *Her* is the pronoun object of the preposition *with.*

IN GERMAN

As in English, prepositions never change form. Unlike English, however, the noun or pronoun object of the preposition will be in the accusative, dative, or genitive case depending on the preposition. Be sure to learn the meaning and use of each German preposition, as well as the case that must follow it (see also *What is an Object of a Preposition Pronoun?*, p. 67).

Below are examples of various prepositions, each requiring a different case.

- **durch** *(through)* → accusative object

  > Er wirft den Ball **durch** das Fenster.
  >
  > accusative
  >
  > *He throws the ball **through** the window.*

- **bei** *(with)* → dative object

  > Er wohnt **bei** seiner Tante.
  >
  > dative
  >
  > *He lives **with** his aunt.*

- **trotz** *(in spite of)* → genitive object

  > **Trotz** des Regens machten wir einen Spaziergang.
  >
  > genitive
  >
  > *In spite of the rain we took a walk.*

TWO-WAY PREPOSITIONS

German also has a group of prepositions called TWO-WAY PREPOSITIONS, so called because they can be followed by either an accusative object or a dative object, depending on the way the preposition is used.

- when used with a verb expressing motion in a particular direction or from one position to another → accusative object

  > *We are driving **into** town tomorrow.*
  >
  > Driving in a particular direction → accusative
  >
  > Wir fahren morgen **in** die Stadt.
  >
  > accusative object

*He lays the book **on** the table.*
Book moved from one position to another → accusative
Er legt das Buch **auf** den Tisch.

accusative object

- when used with a verb expressing location or direction-less motion → dative object

  *Do you live **in** the city?*
  Expressing location, no motion → dative
  Wohnt ihr **in** der Stadt?

  dative object

  *The book lies **on** the table.*
  Expressing location, no motion → dative
  Das Buch liegt **auf** dem Tisch.

  dative object

POSITION OF PREPOSITION AND ITS OBJECT
IN ENGLISH

The position of a preposition in an English sentence is variable. In spoken English a preposition tends to be at the end of the sentence, far from its object; this is called a DANGLING PREPOSITION. Restructuring the sentence so that the preposition is placed before its object, as is the tendency in formal English, will help you identify the words as a prepositional phrase.

SPOKEN ENGLISH   →   FORMAL ENGLISH
Who did you get the book from?   *From whom did you get the book?*

object *(whom)*   preposition   object of preposition *from*

IN GERMAN

There are no dangling prepositions. Nearly all German prepositions are placed as they are in formal English, that is, either beside their object within the sentence or at the beginning of a question.

*Who are you leaving **with**?* →
***With whom** are you leaving?*
Mit wem gehst du?

preposition + object

*Who did you get the book **from**?* →
***From whom** did you get the book?*
Von wem hast du das Buch bekommen?

preposition + object

Your textbook will indicate the few prepositions that must or can follow their objects.

The position of prepositions in German sentences enables us to distinguish them from separable prefixes (see *What are Prefixes and Suffixes?*, p. 31). For instance, when placed at the end of the sentence and not next to their object, **mit, vor,** and **an** are the separable prefixes of the verbs **mitkommen** *(to come along),* **vorkommen** *(to happen),* and **anhalten** *(to stop).*

130

> Wer **kommt mit?**
> *Who is **coming along?***
>
> Das **kommt** manchmal **vor.**
> *That **happens** sometimes.*
>
> Der Zug **hält** in München **an.**
> *The train **stops** in Munich.*

CAREFUL — Prepositions are tricky, because every language uses prepositions differently. Do not assume that the same preposition is used in German as in English, or even that a preposition will be needed in German when you must use one in English and vice versa.

140

ENGLISH	MAN
PREPOSITION	NO PREPOSITION
to look *for*	suchen
to look *at*	betrachten
NO PREPOSITION	PREPOSITION
to answer	antworten **auf**
CHANGE OF PREPOSITION	
to protect *from*	schützen **vor** *(before)*
to wait *for*	warten **auf** *(on)*
to die *of*	sterben **an** *(at)*

150

A dictionary will usually give you the verb plus the preposition that follows it, when one is required. Do not translate an English verb + preposition word-for-word. For example, when you consult the dictionary to find the German equivalent of *to talk about,* do not stop at the first entry for *talk* (**sprechen**) and then add the German equivalent of the preposition *about.* Continue searching for the specific meaning *talk about,* which corresponds to the verb **sprechen** with the preposition **über** (meaning *over* or *above*).

160

> *We are talking **about** politics.*
> Wir sprechen **über** Politik.

On the other hand, when looking up a verb such as *to pay for something,* notice that the German equivalent **bezahlen** is used without a preposition.

> *We paid for the meal.*
> Wir **bezahlten** das Essen.

170

Your German textbook will introduce phrases like **warten auf** + accusative object *(to wait for)* and **bitten um** + accusative object *(to ask for)*. Make sure you learn the verb together with the preposition and its case so that you can use the entire pattern correctly.

STUDY TIPS — PREPOSITIONS

Flashcards

1. Create a card for each preposition. On the German side, include the case (Acc., Dat., Acc./Dat., or Gen.) that follows that preposition. Add a sample sentence.
2. Sort the cards according to the case that follows. To remember the case, here are some strategies other learners have used:

   a) Preposition + accusative — Create a phrase or acronym based on the first letter of each preposition in the group **für, durch, gegen, um, ohne** "Furry dogs greet us often" or the acronym "dogfu."

   b) Preposition + dative — Sing the prepositions **aus, außer, bei, mit, nach, seit, von, zu** to a familiar tune. For ex.: in alphabetical order to the tune of the *Blue Danube Waltz*.

   c) Two-way prepositions — Two suggestions:

   - Imagine all the places a house-fly could fly or land in relation to an object, such as a wine glass: **über** *(above)*, **unter** *(below)*, **vor** *(in front of)*, **hinter** *(behind)*, **auf** *(on top of)*, **an** *(up against)*, **in** *(in)*, **neben** *(beside)*, **zwischen** *(between)*.
   - Draw two related pictures. In the first picture, illustrate an object or person moving to a new location *(The cat crawls under a chair.)*. In the second picture, illustrate that object or person in a stationary position *(The cat is sleeping under the chair.)* Under each picture, write the corresponding sentence in German using the correct preposition and case to describe the scene.

WHAT IS AN OBJECT OF PREPOSITION PRONOUN?

Object pronouns are also used as **OBJECTS OF A PREPOSITION**.

> They went out with *me*.
> object of preposition *with*

IN ENGLISH

Object of preposition pronouns are the same as the pronouns used as direct and indirect objects. They can replace any noun object, including persons, things, or ideas (see *What are Direct and Indirect Object Pronouns?*, p. 57).

> The teacher saw *me*.
> direct object
> The teacher gave *me* the book.
> indirect object
> The teacher spoke with *me* after class.
> object of preposition *with*
> The teacher talked about *it* in class.
> object of preposition *about*

IN GERMAN

The objects of prepositions in German can be in the accusative, dative, or genitive case. Normally we replace a noun object with a pronoun only if the noun replaced refers to a person. A different construction is used when the pronoun refers to a thing or idea. Let us look at the two types of constructions.

REFERRING TO A PERSON

When the pronoun object of a preposition refers to a person or an animal, follow the steps you have already learned to choose the appropriate personal pronoun (see p. 24).

1. ANTECEDENT — Find the noun replaced.
2. GENDER — Determine the gender of the antecedent.
3. CASE — Identify the case required by the preposition.
4. SELECTION — Select the appropriate pronoun form from the chart on p. 58.

Below are examples showing how to analyze sentences that have a pronoun referring to a person as the object of a preposition.

Is Anja buying something for her brother?
*Yes, she is buying something **for him**.*
1. ANTECEDENT: brother
2. GENDER: **der Bruder** *(brother)* is masculine.
3. CASE: **für** takes an accusative object
4. SELECTION: masculine accusative → **ihn**

Kauft Anja etwas für ihren Bruder?
Ja, sie kauft etwas **für ihn**.

Did Franz talk about his sister?
*No, he did not talk **about her**.*
1. ANTECEDENT: sister
2. GENDER: **die Schwester** *(sister)* is feminine.
3. CASE: **von** takes a dative object
4. SELECTION: feminine dative → **ihr**

Sprach Franz von seiner Schwester?
Nein, er sprach nicht **von ihr**.

REFERRING TO A THING

To replace a pronoun object of a preposition whose antecedent is a thing or idea, German uses a construction called the **DA-COMPOUND**. It is formed by adding the prefix **da-** to the preposition, or **dar-** if the preposition begins with a vowel.

Let us look at some examples.:

*Are you thinking **about the price**? Don't think **about it**.*
Denken Sie **an den Preis**? Denken Sie nicht **daran**!

      preposition noun   da-construction:
               (a thing)   **da- + -r- +** preposition **an**

*Does Beth talk **about her courses**? Yes, she does talk **about them**.*
Spricht Beth **von ihren Kursen**? Ja, sie spricht **davon**.

        preposition   noun   da-construction:
                 (a thing)   **da- +** preposition **von**

Your German textbook will discuss this construction and its use in greater detail.

STUDY TIPS — OBJECT OF PREPOSITION PRONOUNS

Pattern

Let's compare **da-** to **wo-**compounds (see *What is an Interrogative Pronoun?*, p. 70) to find similarities in form and usage.

Compare forms

wo-compound	da-compound
woran	daran
worin	darin
wofür	dafür
womit	damit

Compare usage

Both used when anticipating or referring to a thing or an idea, not a person.

wo-compound in questions	da-compound in statement
Worauf wartest du?	
Wartest du **auf den Bus**?	Nein, **darauf** warte ich nicht.
*What are you waiting **for**?*	
*Are you waiting **for the bus**?*	*No, I'm not waiting **for it**.*

CHAPTER

WHAT IS AN INTERROGATIVE PRONOUN?

An **INTERROGATIVE PRONOUN** is a word that replaces a noun and introduces a question. The word *interrogative* comes from *interrogate,* to question.

> *Who* is coming for dinner?
> question referring to a person

> *What* did you eat for dinner?
> question referring to a thing

In both English and German, a different interrogative pronoun is used depending on whether it refers to a "person" (human beings, and live animals) or a "thing" (objects and ideas). Also, the form of the interrogative pronoun often changes according to its function in the sentence: subject, direct object, indirect object, and object of a preposition. We shall look at each type separately.

REFERRING TO A PERSON
IN ENGLISH

There are three interrogative pronouns referring to persons.

Who is used for the subject of the sentence (see *What is a Subject?*, p. 41).

> *Who* lives here?
> subject

> *Who* are they?
> subject

Whom is used for the direct object, indirect object, and object of a preposition (see *What is an Object?*, p. 53 and p. 62 in *What is a Preposition?*).

> *Whom* do you know here?
> direct object

> *To whom* did you speak?
> indirect object

> *From whom* did you get the book?
> object of preposition *from*

CAREFUL — In spoken English we often use the interrogative pronoun *who* instead of *whom*. This makes it difficult to identify its function: is it the subject or an object? It is only by asking the proper questions that you will find the function.

> *Who* do you know here?
> VERB: know
> SUBJECT: Who knows? *You* → subject
> FUNCTION OF *who*: object
> *Whom* do you know here?

Whose, the possessive form, is used to ask about possession or ownership.

> There's a pencil on the floor? *Whose* is it?
> |
> possessive

> They are nice cars. *Whose* are they?
> |
> possessive

IN GERMAN

There are four forms of interrogative pronouns depending on the case required. Number and gender do not affect interrogative pronouns in German.

To select the proper form of the interrogative pronoun you will have to determine its function in the German sentence by asking the following five questions:

1. Is it the subject of the question?
2. Is it the object of the German verb? Does that verb take the accusative or dative object?
3. Is it the indirect object of the German verb?
4. Is it the object of a preposition? If so, does that German preposition take the accusative or dative?
5. Is it the possessive pronoun *whose?*

Subject — *who?* → (nom.) **wer?** — can refer to both singular and plural subjects.

> *Who is in the room? The teacher is in the room.*
> **Wer** ist in dem Zimmer? Die Lehrerin ist in dem Zimmer.

> *Who is coming this evening? Hans and Anja are coming.*
> **Wer** kommt heute abend? Hans und Anja kommen.

Object — *whom?* → (acc.) **wen?** or (dat.) **wem?** — depending on the case required in German.

> *Whom do you see?*
> **Wen** sehen Sie?
> |
> direct object → accusative

For whom is the letter?
Für wen ist der Brief?

preposition **für** *(for)* → accusative object

To whom did you tell the story?
Wem hast du die Geschichte erzählt?

indirect object → dative

With whom are you coming?
Mit wem kommst du?

preposition **mit** *(with)* → dative object

Whom are they helping?
Wem helfen sie?

verb **helfen** *(to help)* → dative direct object

REFERRING TO A THING
IN ENGLISH

There is one interrogative pronoun referring to things or ideas.

What is used for subject, direct object, indirect object, and the object of a preposition.

What happened?

subject

What do you want?

direct object

What is the movie about?

object of preposition *about*

IN GERMAN

As in English, there is only one interrogative pronoun referring to things or ideas.

Was *(what)* is used as a subject or a direct object.

Was ist in diesem Paket?
What is in this package?

Was machst du?
What are you doing?

A construction called the **WO-COMPOUND**, formed by adding the prefix **wo-** (**wor-** if the preposition begins with a vowel) to the preposition, is used when *what* is the object of a preposition.

Here are two examples.

> **What** *are you talking* **about?**
> **Wovon** redet ihr?
>
> wo- + von *(about)*

> **What** *is he waiting* **for?**
> **Worauf** wartet er?
>
> wor- + auf *(for)*

130

Your German textbook will discuss this construction and its use in greater detail.

SUMMARY

Here is a chart you can use as reference.

INTERROGATIVE PRONOUN		
REFERRING TO PERSONS		
NOMINATIVE	wer	*who*
ACCUSATIVE	wen	*whom*
DATIVE	wem	*whom*
GENITIVE	wessen	*whose*
REFERRING TO THINGS	was	*what*
	wo(r)- + prep.	

140

STUDY TIPS — INTERROGATIVE PRONOUNS

Patterns

Compare the interrogative pronouns with the masculine forms of other parts of speech, such as personal pronouns and definite articles.

	Interrogative pronoun	Personal pronoun	Definite article
Nom.	wer	er	der
Acc.	wen	ihn	den
Dat.	wem	ihm	dem
Gen.	wessen		des

What similarities do you see?

-r, -n-, -m, -s mark the case of these pronouns and masculine articles.

- nominative forms end in –r
- accusative forms end in –n
- dative forms end in –m
- genitive forms have an –s

Practice

1. On a blank piece of paper write questions using the various German forms.
2. As a separate exercise, write German sentences with different types of objects. Then write the questions one could ask about that statement.

ANSWER: Der Student schreibt seiner Professorin eine Email.
                 The student writes his professor an email.
QUESTION: Wem schreibt der Student eine Email?
                 To whom is he writing an email?
ANSWER: Die Studentin liest ein Buch.
                 The student is reading a book.
QUESTION: Was liest die Studentin?
                 What is she reading?

WHAT IS AN ADJECTIVE?

An **ADJECTIVE** is a word that describes a noun or a pronoun. There are different types of adjectives; they are classified according to the way they describe a noun or pronoun.

DESCRIPTIVE ADJECTIVE — A descriptive adjective indicates a quality; it tells what kind of noun it is (see p. 131).

> She read an *interesting* book.
> He has *brown* eyes.

POSSESSIVE ADJECTIVE — A possessive adjective shows possession; it tells whose noun it is (see p. 83).

> *His* book is lost.
> *Our* parents are away.

INTERROGATIVE ADJECTIVE — An interrogative adjective asks a question about a noun (see p. 78).

> *What* book is lost?
> *Which* book did you read?

DEMONSTRATIVE ADJECTIVE — A demonstrative adjective points out a noun (see p. 76).

> *This* teacher is excellent.
> *That* question is very appropriate.

IN ENGLISH

English adjectives usually do not change their form, regardless of the noun or pronouns described.

IN GERMAN

While English adjectives do not change their form, German adjectives change in order to agree with the case, gender, and number of the noun they modify. The various types of adjectives are discussed in separate sections.

CHAPTER 22

WHAT IS A DEMONSTRATIVE ADJECTIVE?

A **DEMONSTRATIVE ADJECTIVE** is a word used to point out a noun.

> *This* book is interesting.
> |
> points out the noun *book*

IN ENGLISH

The demonstrative adjectives are *this* and *that* in the singular and *these* and *those* in the plural. They are rare examples of English adjectives agreeing in number with the noun they modify: *this* changes to *these* and *that* changes to *those* when they modify a plural noun (see *What is Meant by Number?*, p. 14).

Singular	Plural
this cat	*these* cats
that man	*those* men

This and *these* refer to persons or objects near the speaker, and *that* and *those* refer to persons or objects away from the speaker.

IN GERMAN

The stems of the demonstrative adjectives are **dies-** *(this)*, **jen-** *(that)*, and **jed-** *(every)*. Like all adjectives in German, the ending changes to agree in case, gender, and number with the noun modified. To choose the correct ending:

1. Identify and analyze the noun modified.
   - What is its case?
   - What is its gender?
   - What is its number?
2. Provide the ending that corresponds to the case, gender, and number of the noun modified. These endings are the same as those for the definite articles (**der, die, das**, see p. 18 and p. 39). Because they follow the same pattern as definite articles, your textbook may refer to the demonstrative adjectives as "**der**-words."

Let us apply the above steps to some examples.

> *This room is large.*
> _____ Zimmer ist gross.
>> 1. Noun modified: room
>> Case: subject of **sein** *(to be)* → nominative

GENDER: **das Zimmer** *(room)* → neuter
NUMBER: **das Zimmer** *(room)* → singular
2. ENDING: nominative neuter singular ending → **-es**

Dieses Zimmer ist gross. [40]

*Show **every** person the house.*
Zeig _____ Person das Haus.

1. NOUN MODIFIED: person
CASE: indirect object of **zeigen** *(to show)* → dative
GENDER: **die Person** *(person)* → feminine
NUMBER: **die Person** *(person)* → singular
2. ENDING: dative feminine singular ending → **-er**

Zeig **jeder** Person das Haus.

CHAPTER

WHAT IS AN INTERROGATIVE ADJECTIVE?

An **INTERROGATIVE ADJECTIVE** is a word that asks for information about a noun.

> *Which* book do you want?
>
> asks information about the noun *book*

IN ENGLISH

The words *which* and *what* are called interrogative adjectives when they come in front of a noun and are used to ask a question about that noun.

> *Which* instructor is teaching the course?
> *What* courses are you taking?

IN GERMAN

The stem of the interrogative adjective is **welch-** *(which, what)*. Like all adjectives in German, the ending changes to agree in case, gender, and number with the noun modified. To choose the correct ending:

1. Identify and analyze the noun modified.
   - What is its case?
   - What is its gender?
   - What is its number?
2. Provide the ending that corresponds to the case, gender, and number of the noun modified. These endings are the same as those for the definite articles (**der, die, das**, see p. 18 and p. 39). Because they follow the same pattern as definite articles, except in the neuter singular nominative and accusative where the ending -es replaces -as, your textbook may refer to **welch-** as a "**der**-word."

Let us apply the above steps to examples.

> ***Which** lamp is cheaper?*
> _____ Lampe ist billiger?
> 1. NOUN MODIFIED: lamp
>   CASE: subject of **sein** *(to be)* → nominative
>   GENDER: **die Lampe** *(lamp)* → feminine
>   NUMBER: *lamp* → singular
> 2. ENDING: nominative feminine singular → -e
> **Welche** Lampe ist billiger?

Which (what) dress do you want to wear?
_____ Kleid willst du tragen?

> 1. NOUN MODIFIED: dress
>   CASE: direct object of **tragen** *(to wear)* → accusative
>   GENDER: **das Kleid** *(dress)* → neuter
>   NUMBER: *dress* → singular
> 2. ENDING: accusative neuter singular → **-es**

Welches Kleid willst du tragen?

Which man do we give our tickets to?
_____ Mann geben wir unsere Karten?

> 1. NOUN MODIFIED: man
>   CASE: indirect object of **geben** *(to give)* → dative
>   GENDER: **der Mann** *(man)* → masculine
>   NUMBER: *man* → singular
> 2. ENDING: dative masculine singular → **-em**

Welchem Mann geben wir unsere Karten?

AS OBJECT OF A PREPOSITION

When expressing an English question with an interrogative adjective, be sure to restructure any dangling preposition (see p. 64). Begin the question with the preposition, followed by the interrogative adjective in the case required by that preposition (see pp. 63-4).

*Which street does he live **on**? → **On which** street does he live?*
_____ Straße wohnt er?

> 1. NOUN MODIFIED: street
>   CASE: object of preposition **in** *(in, on)* → dative
>   GENDER: **die Straße** *(street)* → feminine
>   NUMBER: *street* → singular
> 2. ENDING: dative feminine singular → **-er**

In welcher Straße wohnt er?

***What** film are you talking **about**? → **About what** film are you talking?*
_____ Film sprecht ihr?

> 1. NOUN MODIFIED: film
>   CASE: object of preposition **von** *(about)* → dative
>   GENDER: **der Film** *(film)* → masculine
>   NUMBER: *film* → singular
> 2. ENDING: dative masculine singular → **-em**

Von welchem Film sprecht ihr?

CAREFUL — The word *what* is not always an interrogative adjective. It can also be an interrogative pronoun (see *What is an Interrogative Pronoun?*, p. 70). When it is a pronoun, *what* is not followed by a noun.

What is on the table?

interrogative pronoun

Was ist auf dem Tisch?

It is important that you distinguish interrogative adjectives from interrogative pronouns because, in German, different words are used and they follow different rules.

WHAT IS A POSSESSIVE PRONOUN?

A **POSSESSIVE PRONOUN** is a word that replaces a noun and indicates the possessor of that noun. The word *possessive* comes
from *possess,* to own.

> Whose house is that? It's *mine.*
>
> replaces the noun *house,* the object possessed,
> and shows who possesses it, *me.*

IN ENGLISH

Like subject pronouns, possessive pronouns are identified
according to the person they represent (see p. 23).

SINGULAR POSSESSOR

1ST PERSON		mine
2ND PERSON		yours
3RD PERSON	MASCULINE	his
	FEMININE	hers
	NEUTER	its

PLURAL POSSESSOR

1ST PERSON	ours
2ND PERSON	yours
3RD PERSON	theirs

The pronouns refer to the possessor, not the possessed.

> My car is red; what color is Niko's? *His* is blue.
>
> 3rd pers. masc. sing.

> Niko's car is blue. What color is yours? *Mine* is white.
>
> 1st pers. sing.

> Although the object possessed is the same *(car),* different
> possessive pronouns *(his* and *mine)* are used because the
> possessors are different *(Niko* and *me).*

> Is that Niko's house? Yes, it is *his.*
> Are those Niko's keys? Yes, they are *his.*

> Although the objects possessed are different *(house* and
> *keys),* the same possessive pronoun *(his)* is used because
> the possessor is the same *(Niko).*

1

10

20

30

IN GERMAN

Like English, a German possessive pronoun refers to the
possessor. Unlike English, however, and like all German
pronouns, possessive pronouns also agree in gender and
number with the antecedent, that is, with the person or
object possessed. In addition, the appropriate case endings
are added to the possessive pronoun to reflect its function
in the sentence.

Let us look at the German possessive pronouns to which
the case endings are added.

SINGULAR POSSESSOR

1ST PERSON		mein-	*mine*
2ND PERSON	INFORMAL	dein-	*yours*
	FORMAL	Ihr-	*yours*
3RD PERSON	MASCULINE	sein-	*his*
	FEMININE	ihr-	*hers*
	NEUTER	sein-	*its*

PLURAL POSSESSOR

1ST PERSON		unser-	*ours*
2ND PERSON	INFORMAL	euer-	*yours*
	FORMAL	Ihr-	*yours*
3RD PERSON		ihr-	*theirs*

The case endings of possessive pronouns are essentially
the same as those of the possessive adjectives (see p. 84 in
What is a Possessive Adjective?). Possessive adjectives are
more commonly used in German than the possessive pronoun. Your textbook will explain how to recognize possessive pronouns.

WHAT IS A POSSESSIVE ADJECTIVE?

A **POSSESSIVE ADJECTIVE** is a word that describes a noun   1
by showing who possesses that noun.

> Whose house is that? It's *my* house.
>
> describes the noun *house*,
> and shows who possesses it, *me*

IN ENGLISH

Like subject pronouns, possessive adjectives are identified
according to the person they represent (see p. 23).

Singular possessor		
1ˢᵀ PERSON		my
2ᴺᴰ PERSON		your
	MASCULINE	his
3ᴿᴰ PERSON	FEMININE	her
	NEUTER	its

10

Plural possessor	
1ˢᵀ PERSON	our
2ᴺᴰ PERSON	your
3ᴿᴰ PERSON	their

A possessive adjective changes to identify the possessor,   20
regardless of the objects possessed.

> Is that Niko's house? Yes, it is *his* house.
> Is that Ingrid's house? Yes, it is *her* house.
>> Although the object possessed is the same *(house)*, different
>> possessive adjectives *(his* and *her)* are used because the pos-
>> sessors are different *(Niko* and *Ingrid)*.
>
> Is that Niko's house? Yes, it is *his* house.
> Are those Niko's keys? Yes, they are *his* keys.
>> Although the objects possessed are different *(house* and
>> *keys)*, the same possessive adjective *(his)* is used because the   30
>> possessor is the same *(Niko)*.

IN GERMAN

Like English, a German possessive adjective changes to
identify the possessor, but unlike English it also agrees in
case, gender, and number with the noun possessed. To
choose the correct form of the possessive adjective follow
these steps:

1. Find the possessor.

SINGULAR POSSESSOR			
1ST PERSON		mein-	*my*
2ND PERSON	FAMILIAR	dein-	*your*
	FORMAL	Ihr	*your*
	MASCULINE	sein-	*his*
3RD PERSON	FEMININE	ihr-	*her*
	NEUTER	sein-	*its*

PLURAL POSSESSOR			
1ST PERSON		unser-	*our*
2ND PERSON	FAMILIAR	euer-	*your*
	FORMAL	Ihr-	*your*
3RD PERSON		ihr-	*their*

2. Identify and analyze the noun possessed.
   - What is its case?
   - What is its gender?
   - What is its number?
3. Provide the ending that corresponds to the case, gender, and number of the noun possessed. These endings are the same as those for the indefinite articles (**ein, eine, ein,** see p. 19 and p. 39). Because they follow the same pattern as indefinite articles, your textbook may refer to possessive adjectives as "**ein**-words."

Let us apply the above steps to examples.

> *He always forgets **his** books.*
> Er vergißt immer _____ Bücher.
> > 1. POSSESSOR: *his* → **sein-**
> > 2. NOUN POSSESSED: *books*
> >   CASE: **vergessen** *(to forget)* takes a direct object → accusative
> >   GENDER: **das Buch** *(book)* → neuter
> >   NUMBER: *books* → plural
> > 3. ENDING: accusative neuter plural → **-e**
> Er vergißt immer **seine** Bücher.

> *She gives **her** brother the telephone number.*
> Sie gibt _____ Bruder die Telefonnummer.
> > 1. POSSESSOR: *her* → **ihr-**
> > 2. NOUN POSSESSED: *brother*
> >   CASE: indirect object of **geben** *(to give)* → dative
> >   (She gives the number *to whom?* Her brother.)
> >   GENDER: **der Bruder** *(brother)* → masculine
> >   NUMBER: *brother* → singular
> > 3. ENDING: dative masculine singular → **-em**
> Sie gibt **ihrem** Bruder die Telefonnummer.

CAREFUL — Remember that **ihr-** with an ending and followed by a noun is a possessive adjective that can mean *her* or *their* depending on possessor. If **ihr** has no ending and is not in front of a noun, it is a pronoun and it can mean either *you* (nominative, familiar plural) or *her* (dative singular).

80

STUDY TIPS — POSSESSIVE ADJECTIVES

Flashcard

Make a flashcard for each possessive pronoun. On the German side, write the possessive adjective with a dash following it to indicate that an ending it needed. On the English side, write the translation.

unser-	*our*
ihr-	*her, their*

Pattern

Review the case endings for indefinite articles p. 39 in *What is Meant by Case?*. These are the endings for possessive adjectives.

CHAPTER

WHAT IS THE POSSESSIVE?

The **POSSESSIVE** is used to show that one noun *possesses* or owns another noun.

Ingrid's German book is on the table.

noun   noun
possessor   possessed

IN ENGLISH

There are two constructions to show possession.

Apostrophe — In this construction the possessor comes before the noun possessed.

- a singular possessor adds an apostrophe + "s"

    Gabi*'s* mother

    the professor*'s* book

    singular possessor

- a plural possessor ending with "s" adds an apostrophe after the "s"

    the girls' father

    the boys' school

    plural possessor

- a plural possessor not ending with "s" adds an apostrophe + "s"

    the children*'s* playground

    the women*'s* role

    plural possessor

The word "of" — In this construction the noun possessed comes before the possessor.

- a singular or plural possessor is preceded by *of the* or *of a*

    the book *of the* professor

    the branches *of a* tree

    singular possessor

    the teacher *of the* students

    plural possessor

- a proper noun possessor is preceded by *of*

    the poetry *of* Goethe

    proper noun possessor

IN GERMAN

There are also two ways to show possession: the genitive case is used in writing and in formal language and **von +** the dative is used in spoken German.

Genitive case — When the genitive case of a noun is used to show possession, the order in which the noun possessor and the noun possessed appear is different depending on whether the noun possessor is a proper or a common noun.

- proper noun possessor — This German structure parallels the English structure that uses the apostrophe to show possession. Just as in English, the noun possessor, in this case a proper noun, comes before the noun possessed.

  Inges Mutter
  Inge's mother
  possessor possessed

In German the only time that an apostrophe is used for the genitive is when a proper noun ends in -**s** or -**z**.

  Kiwus' Gedichte
  Kiwus's poems
  possessor possessed

- common noun possessor — This German structure parallels the English structure that uses *of the*. Just as in English, the noun possessor, in this case a common noun, generally follows the noun possessed.

Most masculine and neuter singular nouns of one syllable → add -**es**. Masculine and neuter singular nouns of more than one syllable → add -**s**. The accompanying articles also end in -**s** (see pp. 38-9).

  der Ball des Kind**es**
  possessed | possessor
  ball | child
  | neuter singular
  | one syllable **Kind**
  genitive
  definite article

  *the ball **of the** child*
  the child's ball

40

50

60

70

Feminine singular and plural nouns → add **-er** to the preceding article or adjectives. The noun itself has no special ending.

der Mantel de**r** Frau

possessed	possessor
coat	*woman*
	feminine

genitive
definite article

*the coat **of the** woman*
the woman's coat

Your German textbook will explain the genitive in greater detail and will point out the few irregularities.

Von + dative — When the construction **von** + dative case is used to show possession, the same construction is used for proper and common noun possessor. The order in which the noun possessor and the noun possessed appear corresponds to the construction *of* + noun possessor in English.

der Vater **von den** Mädchen

von + dative

*the father **of the** girls*

die Mutter **von** Inge
*the mother **of** Inge*

WHAT IS A SENTENCE?

A **SENTENCE** is a group of words that act together as a complete unit. Typically a sentence consists of at least a subject and a verb (see *What is a Subject?*, p. 41 and *What is a Verb?*, p. 27).

> The girls ran.
> subject verb

> They were eating.
> subject   verb

Depending on the verb, a sentence may also have direct and indirect objects (see *What is an Object?*, p. 53).

> The boy threw the ball.
> subject verb   direct object

> Gabi threw her brother the ball.
> subject verb indirect object   direct object

In addition, a sentence may include other words giving additional information about the subject, verb, or objects; these words are called **MODIFIERS**. There are various kinds of modifiers.

- adjective (see *What is an Adjective?*, p. 75)

> I saw a *great* movie.
> adjective

- adverb (see *What is an Adverb?*, p. 139)

> *Yesterday* I saw a great movie.
> adverb

- prepositional phrase; that is, a group of words that begins with a preposition (see *What is a Preposition?*, p. 62)

> Yesterday *after work* I saw a great movie.
> prepositional phrase modifying *saw*

- participial phrase; that is, a group of words that begins with a participle (see *What is a Participle?*, p. 116)

> *Attracted by the reviews*, I saw a great movie yesterday.
> participial phrase modifying *I*

- infinitive phrase; that is, a clause that begins with an infinitive (see *What is an Infinitive?*, p. 29).

> *To entertain myself*, I saw a movie.
> └──────┬──────┘
>   infinitive phrase

It is important for you to learn to recognize the different types of sentences, clauses, modifiers, and phrases, since in German they affect the order in which words appear in a sentence.

SIMPLE SENTENCES

A **SIMPLE SENTENCE** is a sentence consisting of only one **CLAUSE,** namely, a group of words including a subject and a conjugated verb.

IN ENGLISH

There is no set position for the verb in an English sentence or clause, but the subject almost always comes before the verb.

> We are going to the concert.
> │ └──┬──┘
> subject verb

A modifier can also come before the subject.

> *Today* we are going to a concert.
> │
> adverb

> *After the party* we are going to a concert.
> └──────┬──────┘
> prepositional phrase modifying *are going*

IN GERMAN

In a simple sentence the conjugated verb always stands in second position.

> Wir **gehen** in ein Konzert.
> *we **are going** to a   concert*
> │   └──┬──┘
> subject verb
> 1   2

> Heute **gehen** wir in ein Konzert.
> *today **are going** we to a   concert*
> │   │   │
> adverb verb subject
> 1   2
> *Today we **are going** to a concert.*

This does not mean that the verb is always the second word in the sentence, because some groups of words, such as prepositional phrases, together count as one position.

Nach der Party **gehen** wir in ein Konzert. 80
after the party ***are going*** *we to a concert*
⎣_____⎦ ⎣_____⎦ |
prep. phrase verb subject
1 2
*After the party we **are going** to a concert.*

As you can see above, only in the first example is it possible to put the subject before the verb. In the other two sentences where there is a modifier, the subject must follow the verb.

COMPOUND SENTENCES

90

A COMPOUND SENTENCE consists of two equal clauses, each with a subject and a conjugated verb, joined by a coordinating conjunction (see *What is a Conjunction?*, p. 127). In both English and German the word order of each clause is the same as for any simple sentence.

IN ENGLISH

As in simple sentences, the position of the verb can vary, though the subject (S) usually comes before the verb (V).

clause 1   clause 2
The sky is gray, *but* it is not raining. 100
  S   V | S V
      coordinating
      conjunction

clause 1   clause 2
Every evening Max plays the piano *and* his sister sings.
        S   V   S   V
                coordinating
                conjunction

IN GERMAN

It is important that you know how to recognize a compound sentence because the verb is in the second position of each clause. The coordinating conjunction is just a link between the two simple sentences and does not count as the first position.

110

Der Himmel **ist** grau, aber es **regnet** nicht.
     | | | | |
     1   2   conj. 1   2
the sky ***is*** *gray, but it* ***is raining*** *not*
*The sky **is** gray, but it **is** not **raining.***

Jeden Abend **spielt** Max Klavier und seine Schwester **singt**.
⎣_____⎦ | | ⎣_____⎦ |
     1   2   conj.   1   2
every evening ***plays*** *Max the piano and* *his sister* ***sings*** 120
*Every evening Max **plays** the piano and his sister **sings**.*

COMPLEX SENTENCES

A **COMPLEX SENTENCE** is a sentence consisting of a main clause and one or more dependent clauses.

The **MAIN CLAUSE**, also called an **INDEPENDENT CLAUSE**, is a clause that could stand alone as a complete sentence.

The **DEPENDENT CLAUSE**, also called a **SUBORDINATE CLAUSE**, cannot stand alone as a complete sentence because it depends on the main clause for its full meaning.

dependent clause   main clause

Before I eat, I always wash my hands.

> It makes sense to say "I always wash my hands" without the first clause in the sentence; therefore, it is the main clause. It does not make sense to say, "before I eat" unless we add a conclusion; therefore, it is the dependent clause.

IN ENGLISH

Distinguishing a main clause from a dependent clause helps you to write complete sentences and avoid sentence fragments.

IN GERMAN

It is important for you to learn to distinguish between a main clause and a dependent clause, because each type of clause has its own word order rules.

Main clause — The word order depends on whether the main clause is at the beginning of the sentence or at the end.

- at the beginning of the sentence — the verb of the main clause remains in the same position as in the simple sentence; that is, in the second position.

     main clause   dependent clause

Ich **wasche** mir immer die Hände, bevor ich esse.
    1   2

I   **wash** *myself always the hands*   *before I*   *eat*
*I always **wash** my hands before I eat.*

- at the end of the sentence — the verb of the main clause comes right after the dependent clause that functions as a single unit of meaning and counts as the first position.

dependent clause   main clause

Bevor ich esse, **wasche** ich mir immer die Hände.
     1   2

before *I* *eat*   **wash** *I* *myself always the hands*
*Before I eat, I always **wash** my hands.*

Dependent clause — the conjugated verb always stands at the end of the dependent clause, regardless if it comes before or after the main clause.

main clause	dependent clause

Ich wasche mir die Hände, weil sie schmutzig **sind**.

I   wash   myself the hands   because they dirty   are
*I wash my hands, because they **are** dirty.*

170

Your German textbook will explain this structure in more detail.

WHAT ARE AFFIRMATIVE AND
NEGATIVE SENTENCES?

¹ A sentence can be classified according to whether or not the verb is negated, that is, made negative with the word *not*.

An **AFFIRMATIVE SENTENCE** is a sentence whose verb is not negated. It states a fact that is.

> Austria is a country in Europe.
> Gabi will work at the university.
> They liked to travel.

A **NEGATIVE SENTENCE** is a sentence whose verb is negated with the word *not*. It states a fact that is not.

¹⁰
> Austria is *not* a country in Asia.
> Gabi will *not* work at the university.
> They *did not* like to travel.

IN ENGLISH

An affirmative sentence can be made negative in one of two ways:

- by adding *not* after auxiliary verbs or modals (see *What is an Auxiliary Verb?*, p. 105)

²⁰
AFFIRMATIVE	NEGATIVE
Axel *is* a student.	Axel is *not* a student.
Gabi *can* do it.	Gabi can*not* do it.
They *will* travel.	They will *not* travel.

The word *not* is often attached to the auxiliary and the letter "o" replaced by an apostrophe; this is called a **CONTRACTION**: is not → isn't; cannot → can't; will not → won't.

- by adding the auxiliary verb *do, does,* or *did* + *not* followed by the dictionary form of the main verb

AFFIRMATIVE	NEGATIVE
We *study* a lot.	We *do not* study a lot.
Max *writes* well.	Max *does not* write well.
³⁰ | The train *arrived*. | The train *did not* arrive. |

The words *do, does, did* are often contracted with *not*: do not → don't; does not → doesn't; did not → didn't.

IN GERMAN

Unlike English that always uses *not* to make an affirmative sentence negative, German uses either **nicht** or **kein** depending on the part of speech being negated.

■ to negate verbs and other parts of speech → **nicht** *(not)*

Nicht never changes form, but its position in the sentence varies: **nicht** follows all personal pronouns, the subject, verb, direct object, and expressions of definite time, and precedes everything else in the sentence. Let's look at some examples.

AFFIRMATIVE	**NEGATIVE**
Ich sehe dich.	Ich sehe dich **nicht**.
	personal pronoun + **nicht**
I see you.	*I **don't** see you.*
Er arbeitet in Berlin.	Er arbeitet **nicht** in Berlin.
	verb + **nicht** + prepositional phrase
He works in Berlin.	*He **doesn't** work in Berlin.*
Sie besucht Anna oft.	Sie besucht Anna **nicht** oft.
	direct object + **nicht** + adverb
She visits Anna often.	*She **doesn't** visit Anna often.*
Er kommt morgen abend.	Er kommt morgen abend **nicht**.
	definite time + **nicht**
He is coming tomorrow night.	*He is **not** coming tomorrow night.*

Your textbook will discuss the position of **nicht** in greater detail.

■ to negate a non-specific noun; i.e., a noun preceded by an indefinite article or no article → **kein** *(not a, not any, no)*

Kein agrees in gender, number, and case with the noun it precedes and takes the same endings as **ein**-words (see p. 39).

AFFIRMATIVE	**NEGATIVE**
Anna sieht **einen** Hund.	Anna sieht **keinen Hund**.
indefinite article	masc. sing. acc. (direct object)
*Anna sees **a** dog.*	*Anna sees **no dog**.*
	[Anna doesn't see a dog.]
Ich habe Zeit.	Ich habe **keine Zeit**.
no article	fem. sing. acc. (direct object)
I have time.	*I have **no time**.*
	[I don't have time.]
Studenten wohnen hier.	**Keine Studenten** wohnen hier.
no article	masc. pl. nom. (subject)
Students live here.	***No students** live here.*

40

50

60

70

CAREFUL — Remember that in negative sentences in German there is no equivalent for the auxiliary words *do, does, did*; do not try to include them.

NEGATIVE WORDS
In both English and German there are other negative words besides *not* that can be added to an affirmative sentence.

IN ENGLISH
The most common negative words are *nothing, nobody, no one,* which can be used as subjects or objects of a sentence.

> *Nothing* is free.
> *Nobody* is going to the movies.
> |
> subject
>
> I see *nothing*.
> I see *no one (nobody)*.
> |
> object

IN GERMAN
The most common negative words are **nichts** *(nothing)* and **niemand** *(no one, nobody)*. As in English they can be used as subjects or objects of a sentence.

- subject of the sentence

> **Nichts** ist umsonst.
> *Nothing is free.*
> **Niemand** geht ins Kino.
> *No one is going to the movies.*

- object of the sentence — **nichts** doesn't change regardless of its function; **niemand** as an object can be either in the accusative (**-en**) or the dative (**-em**) depending on the verb.

> Ich sehe **nichts**.
> *I see **nothing**.*
> Ich sehe **niemanden**.
> |
>   **sehen** *(to see)* takes an accusative object
> *I see **no one**.*
>
> Er hilft **niemandem**.
> |
>   **helfen** *(to help)* takes dative object
> *He helps **no one**.*

CAREFUL — Note the spelling difference between **nicht** *(not)* and **nichts** *(nothing)*.

WHAT ARE DECLARATIVE AND INTERROGATIVE SENTENCES?

A sentence can be classified as to whether it is making a statement or asking a question.

A **DECLARATIVE SENTENCE** is a sentence that makes a statement.

> Franz arrived in Frankfurt at 11:15 A.M.

An **INTERROGATIVE SENTENCE** is a sentence that asks a question.

> Did Franz arrive in Frankfurt at 11:15 A.M?
> When did Franz arrive in Frankfurt?

In written language, an interrogative sentence always ends with a question mark.

IN ENGLISH

There are two types of interrogative sentences: questions that can be answered by "yes" or "no" and questions that ask for information.

Yes-or-no questions — Questions are formed from a declarative sentence in one of two ways:

- by adding the auxiliary verb *do, does,* or *did* before the subject + the dictionary form of the main verb.

DECLARATIVE SENTENCE	INTERROGATIVE SENTENCE
Ingrid *likes* the class.	*Does* Ingrid *like* the class?
Axel and Julia *sing* well.	*Do* Axel and Julia *sing* well?
Franz *went* to Berlin.	*Did* Franz *go* to Berlin?

- by inverting the normal word order of subject + verb to verb + subject. This **INVERSION** can only be used with auxiliary verbs or auxiliary words (see *What is an Auxiliary Verb?*, p. 105).

DECLARATIVE SENTENCE	INTERROGATIVE SENTENCE
Franz is home.	*Is* Franz home?
subject + verb *to be*	verb + subject
You have received a letter.	*Have you received* a letter?
subject + *have* + main verb	*have* + subject + main verb
She will come tomorrow.	*Will she come* tomorrow?
subject + *will* + main verb	*will* + subject + main verb

₁

₁₀

₂₀

₃₀

Asking for information — Questions start with a question word, such as *when, who, which,* and *how,* + the interrogative sentence as formed above under 1 and 2.

interrogative sentence

Why does Julia like the class?
Where did Ingrid go?

IN GERMAN

As in English, there are two types of interrogative sentences: yes-or-no questions and question word questions.

Yes-or-no questions — Questions are formed by the inversion process, i.e., by moving the conjugated verb from its second position in a declarative sentence to the first position and following it with the subject.

DECLARATIVE SENTENCE	INTERROGATIVE SENTENCE
Julia hat den Kurs **gern**.	**Hat Julia** den Kurs **gern**?
subject + conjugated verb 2nd position	conjugated verb 1st position + subject
Julia likes the class.	*Does Julia like the class?*
Morgen **kommt** sie wieder.	**Kommt sie** morgen wieder?
verb 2nd position + subject	verb 1st position + subject
She is coming again tomorrow.	*Is she coming again tomorrow?*

Asking for information — Questions start with a question word, such as **wann** *(when),* **wo** *(where),* **warum** *(why),* **wie oft** *(how often),* + the interrogative sentence as formed above.

interrogative sentence

Warum hat Julia den Kurs gern?
Why does Julia like the class?

interrogative sentence

Wann kommt sie wieder?
When is she coming?

CAREFUL — Remember that in interrogative sentences there is no equivalent for the auxiliary words *do, does, did* in German; do not try to include them.

TAG QUESTIONS

In both English and German when you expect a yes-or-no answer, you can also transform a statement into a question by adding a short phrase called a TAG at the end of the statement.

IN ENGLISH

The tense of the statement dictates the tense of the tag and affirmative statements take negative tags and negative statements take affirmative tags (see *What are Affirmative and Negative Sentences?*, p. 94).

      affirmative statement   negative tag
Axel and Ingrid *are* friends, *aren't they?*
         present   present
Axel and Ingrid *were* friends, *weren't they?*
         past   past

      negative statement   affirmative tag
Axel and Ingrid *aren't* friends, *are they?*
         present   present
Axel and Ingrid *weren't* friends, *were they?*
         past   past

IN GERMAN

When confirmation is expected, the words **nicht wahr** or **oder** can be added to a statement. **Oder** can be used with either positive or negative statements, but **nicht wahr** is used only with positive statements.

Du kommst heute nicht mit, **oder?**
You aren't coming along today, **are you?**

affirmative statement
Sie wohnt in Berlin, **nicht wahr?**
She lives in Berlin, **doesn't she?**

CHAPTER

WHAT IS THE IMPERATIVE?

The **IMPERATIVE** is used to give someone an order.

> *Come* here!
> *Don't come* here!

IN ENGLISH

There are two types of commands, depending on who is told to do, or not to do, something.

"You" command — When an order is given to one or more persons, the dictionary form of the verb is used.

> *Answer* the phone.
> *Clean* your room.
> *Speak* softly.

"We" command — When an order is given to oneself as well as to others, the phrase "let's" (a contraction of *let us*) is used + the dictionary form of the verb.

> *Let's leave.*
> *Let's go* to the movies.

The absence of the subject pronoun in the sentence is a good indication that you are dealing with an imperative and not a present tense.

> *You answer* the phone.
> └─┬─┘
>   present

> *Answer* the phone.
> │
> imperative

IN GERMAN

As in English, there are two types of imperatives, depending on who is being told to do or not to do something.

"You" command — The *you*-command has three different forms, according to the three different personal pronouns for *you*: familiar **du, ihr**, and formal **Sie** (see *What is a Personal Pronoun?*, p. 23). The verb forms of the imperative are the same as the forms of the present tense indicative, except for the **du**-form. In written German an exclamation mark is used after an imperative.

- **du-form** — When an order is given to a person to whom you say **du**, the imperative is formed by using the stem of the verb; some verbs add the ending -**e**.

  Höre!
  Listen.

  Schreib mir bald!
  Write me soon.

- **ihr-form** — When an order is given to two or more persons to whom you say **du** individually, the form of the verb is the same as the present tense indicative.

  Kommt mit!
  Come along.

  Esst nicht so schnell, Kinder!
  Don't eat so fast, children.

As in English, the subject pronoun is usually dropped in the **du** and **ihr** forms.

- **Sie-form** — When an order is given to one or more persons to whom you say **Sie** individually, the subject pronoun **Sie** is placed directly after the **Sie** form of the verb in the present tense.

  Sprechen Sie lauter!
  Speak more loudly.

  Kommen Sie mit!
  Come along.

"We" command — When an order is given to oneself as well as to others, the subject pronoun **wir** is placed directly after the **wir** form of the verb in the present tense.

  Gehen wir jetzt!
  Let's go now.

  Sprechen wir Deutsch!
  Let's speak German.

Your German textbook will explain in detail the rules for forming the imperative.

CHAPTER

WHAT IS MEANT BY TENSE?

¹ The TENSE of a verb indicates when the action of the verb takes place: at the present time, in the past, or in the future.

I am studying	PRESENT
I studied	PAST
I will study	FUTURE

As you can see in the above examples, just by putting the verb in a different tense, and without giving any additional information (such as "I am studying *now*," "I studied *yesterday*," "I will study *tomorrow*"), you can indicate when the
¹⁰ action of the verb takes place.

Tenses may be classified according to the way they are formed. A SIMPLE TENSE consists of only one verb form (I *studied),* while a COMPOUND TENSE consists of one or more auxiliaries plus the main verb (I *am studying*). See *What is an Auxiliary Verb?*, p. 105.

In this section we will only consider tenses of the indicative mood (see *What is Meant by Mood?*, p. 155).

IN ENGLISH

Listed below are the main tenses of the indicative mood
²⁰ whose equivalents you will encounter in German.

PRESENT
I study	PRESENT
I am studying	PRESENT PROGRESSIVE
I do study	PRESENT EMPHATIC

PAST
I studied	SIMPLE PAST
I did study	PAST EMPHATIC
I have studied	PRESENT PERFECT
I was studying	PAST PROGRESSIVE
³⁰ | I had studied | PAST PERFECT |

FUTURE
I will study	FUTURE
I will have studied	FUTURE PERFECT

As you can see, there are only two simple tenses (present and simple past). All the other tenses are compound tenses.

IN GERMAN

Listed below are the main tenses of the indicative mood that you will encounter in German.

PRESENT

| ich studiere | I study, I do study | PRESENT | 40 |
| | I am studying | | |

PAST

ich studierte	{	I studied,	SIMPLE PAST/
		I was studying	IMPERFECT
ich habe studiert		I have studied	PRESENT PERFECT
ich hatte studiert		I had studied	PAST PERFECT

FUTURE

| ich werde studieren | I will study | FUTURE |
| ich werde studiert haben | I will have studied | FUTURE PERFECT |

As you can see, there are fewer present tense forms in German than in English. The compound tenses in German are formed with the auxiliary verbs **haben** *(to have)* or **sein** *(to be)*, and **werden** *(to become)* + the main verb.

This handbook discusses the various tenses and their usage in separate chapters: *What is the Present Tense?*, p. 104; *What is the Past Tense?*, p. 113; *What is the Future Tense?*, p. 123; *What is the Past Perfect Tense?*, p. 121; and *What is the Future Perfect Tense?*, p. 125. Verb tenses can be grouped according to the mood in which they are used.

CAREFUL — Do not assume that tenses with the same name are used the same way in English and in German.

WHAT IS THE PRESENT TENSE?

The **PRESENT TENSE** indicates that the action is happening at the present time. It can be at the moment the speaker is speaking, a habitual action, or a general truth.

> I *see* you.
> He *smokes* when he *is* nervous.
> The sun *rises* every day.

IN ENGLISH

There are three verb forms that indicate the present tense. Each form has a slightly different meaning:

> Anja *studies* in the library.   PRESENT
> Anja *is studying* in the library.   PRESENT PROGRESSIVE
> Anja *does study* in the library.   PRESENT EMPHATIC

Depending on the way a question is worded, you will automatically choose one of the three above forms.

> Where does Anja study? She *studies* in the library.
> Where is Anja now? She *is studying* in the library.
> Does Anja study in the library? Yes, she *does* [*study* in the library].

IN GERMAN

Unlike English, there is only one verb form to indicate the present tense. The German present tense is used to express the meaning of the English present, present progressive, and present emphatic tenses. The present tense in German is a simple tense formed by adding a set of endings to the stem of the verb (see *What is a Verb Conjugation?*, p. 46). Your textbook will give you the present tense endings.

> Anja *studies* in the library.
>   studiert
>
> Anja *is studying* in the library.
>   studiert
>
> Anja *does study* in the library.
>   studiert

CAREFUL — Remember that in the present tense there is no need for auxiliary verbs such as *is, do, does* in German; do not try to include them.

CHAPTER

33

WHAT IS AN AUXILIARY VERB?

A verb is called an AUXILIARY VERB or HELPING VERB when it
helps another verb, called the MAIN VERB, to form one of its
tenses or alter its meaning.

He *has been gone* two weeks.   *has*   AUXILIARY VERB

                   been   AUXILIARY VERB

                   gone   MAIN VERB

A verb tense composed of an auxiliary verb plus a main verb
is called a COMPOUND TENSE, as opposed to a SIMPLE TENSE that
is a tense composed of only the main verb.

Julia *had studied* for the exam.

      auxiliary   main
      verb   verb
      compound tense

Julia *studies* for the exam.

      simple tense

IN ENGLISH

There are three auxiliary verbs, *to have, to be,* and *to do.*

- auxiliary verbs are used to indicate the tense of the main
  verb.

  Anja *is reading* a book.

  auxiliary *to be* + present participle of *to read*
  present progressive

  Anja *has written* a book.

  auxiliary *to have* + past participle of *to write*
  present perfect

- the auxiliary verb *to do* is used to help formulate questions and to make sentences negative (see *What are
  Declarative and Interrogative Sentences?*, p. 97 and *What
  are Affirmative and Negative Sentences?*, p. 94).

  Does Anja *read* a book?
  Anja *does not read* a book.

- the auxiliary verb *to be* is also used to indicate the verb
  is in the passive voice (see *What is Meant by Active and
  Passive Voice?*, p. 162).

  The book *is read* by many people.

There is also a series of auxiliary words, called MODALS, such as *will, would, may, must, can, could,* that are used to change the tense or meaning of the main verb expressed in its infinitive form.

- the modal *will* is used to indicate the future tense.

    Anja *will read* a book.

    modal *will* + infinitive *read*

- most modals are used to change the meaning of the main verb expressed in its infinitive form.

    Anja *may read* a book.
    Anja *must read* a book.
    Anja *can read* a book.

IN GERMAN

As in English, German has auxiliary verbs and modals.

The three main auxiliary verbs are **haben** *(to have)*, **sein** *(to be)*, and **werden** *(to become)*. As in English, auxiliary verbs are used to indicate the tense of the main verb (see *What is the Past Tense?*, p. 113 and *What is the Future Tense?*, p. 123). The conjugated auxiliary verb is in the second position of the sentence and the past participle or the infinitive form of the main verb is at the end of the sentence (see *What is a Participle?*, p. 116).

Franz **hat** das Buch **gelesen**.

auxiliary **haben** + past participle of **lesen** *(to read)*
present perfect
*Franz **read** the book. [Franz **has read** the book.]*

Franz **wird** das Buch **lesen**.

auxiliary **werden** + infinitive of **lesen**
future
*Franz **will read** the book.*

When **werden** is used as an auxiliary verb, it is not translated in English: with an infinitive it indicates the future tense of the main verb (see the last example above) and with a past participle it indicates the passive voice of the main verb (see p. 164 in *What is Meant by Active and Passive Voice?*).

Das Buch **wird gelesen**.

auxiliary **werden** + past participle of **lesen**
passive voice, present
*The book **is being read**.*

German modals are verbs conjugated in the present and past tenses. As in English, they are used as auxiliaries to change the meaning of the main verb. The modal is in the second position of the sentence and the main verb in the infinitive form is at the end of the sentence.

- **können** *(to be able, can)*
  Lukas **kann** dieses Buch **lesen**.
  *Lukas **can read** this book.*
  [Lukas *has the ability to read* the book.]

- **dürfen** *(to be permitted to, may)*
  Lukas **darf** dieses Buch **lesen**.
  *Lukas **may read** this book.*
  [Lukas *is allowed to read* the book.]

- **müssen** *(to be obligated to, must)*
  Lukas **muss** dieses Buch **lesen**.
  *Lukas **must read** this book.*
  [Lukas *has to read* the book.]

- **sollen** *(to be supposed to, should)*
  Lukas **soll** dieses Buch **lesen**.
  *Lukas **should read** this book.*
  [Lukas *ought to read* the book.]

- **wollen** *(to want to)*
  Lukas **will** dieses Buch **lesen**.
  *Lukas **wants to read** this book.*

CAREFUL — Don't confuse **will**, the 1ˢᵗ and 3ʳᵈ pers. sing. form of the German modal verb **wollen** *(to want)*, and *will*, the English modal that puts the main verb in the future.

Ich **will** gehen.   (**wollen** = *to want to* → MODAL)
*I **want** to go.*

*I **will** go.*
Ich **werde** gehen. (**werden** = *to become* → AUXILIARY TO FORM
FUTURE TENSE)

Consult your textbook for the meaning of German modal verbs and how they are used.

STUDY TIPS — AUXILIARY VERBS

Pattern
Compare the conjugation of modal verbs with the conjugation of regular and stem-changing verbs you learned previously (see p. 50).

REGULAR **wohnen** *(to live)*		STEM-CHANGING **fahren** *(to drive)*		MODAL **können** *(to be able to, can)*		MODAL **müssen** *(to have to, must)*	
wohne	wohnen	fahre	fahren	kann	können	muss	müssen
wohnst	wohnt	fährst	fahrt	kannst	könnt	musst	müsst
wohnt	wohnen	fährt	fahren	kann	können	muss	müssen

What similarities and differences do you see?

1. All verbs: 2nd per. sing. end with -**st**.
2. All verbs: infinitive, 1st and 3rd pers. pl. identical forms.
3. Modal verbs: 1st and 3rd pers. sing. identical.
4. Vowel change: stem-changing verbs have a vowel change in 2nd and 3rd pers. sing. vs. modal verbs have a vowel change in the 1st, 2nd, and 3rd pers. sing.
5. Endings: regular and stem-changing verbs have an ending in the 1st, 2nd, and 3rd pers. sing., vs. modal verbs have no ending in the 1st and 3rd pers. sing., only in the 2nd pers. sing.

Flashcards

Create a flashcard for each modal verb. On the German side, include the conjugation pattern and a sample sentence.

WHAT ARE THE PRINCIPAL PARTS OF A VERB?

The principal parts of a verb are the forms we need to create all the different tenses.

PRESENT	I eat
PRESENT PERFECT	I have eaten
PAST	I ate
PAST PERFECT	I had eaten
FUTURE	I will eat
FUTURE PERFECT	I will have eaten

IN ENGLISH

The principal parts of an English verb are the infinitive *(to eat),* the past tense *(ate),* and the past participle *(eaten).* If you know these parts, you can form all the other tenses of a verb (see *What is Meant by Tense?*, p. 102; *What is the Past Tense?*, p. 113; and *What is a Participle?*, p. 116).

English verbs fall into two categories, depending on how they form their principal parts.

Regular verbs — These verbs are called regular because their past tense and past participle forms follow the predictable pattern of adding *-ed, -d,* or *-t* to the infinitive. They have only two distinct principal parts, the infinitive and the past tense.

INFINITIVE	PAST TENSE/PAST PARTICIPLE
to walk	walk*ed*
to live	liv*ed*
to burn	burn*ed* (burn*t*)

Irregular verbs — These verbs are called irregular because their principal parts do not follow a regular pattern. They have three distinct principal parts, the infinitive, the past tense, and the past participle.

INFINITIVE	PAST TENSE	PAST PARTICIPLE
to sing	sang	sung
to draw	drew	drawn
to hit	hit	hit
to lie	lay	lain
to ride	rode	ridden

IN GERMAN

Regular verbs have the three principal parts: the infinitive, the past tense given in the 3rd person singular, and the past participle. Irregular verbs with a stem vowel change in the 2nd and 3rd person singular of the present tense have a fourth principal part given in the 3rd person singular.

1st PRINCIPAL PART: INFINITIVE	essen	*to eat*
2nd PRINCIPAL PART: PAST TENSE (3rd pers. sing.)	aß	*ate*
3rd PRINCIPAL PART: PAST PARTICIPLE	gegessen	*eaten*
4th PRINCIPAL PART: PRESENT TENSE (3rd pers. sing.)	isst	*eats*

German verbs fall into two categories depending on how they form their principal parts: weak verbs and strong verbs.

REGULAR VERBS ALSO KNOWN AS "WEAK VERBS"

Weak verbs resemble English regular verbs in that the stem of the principal parts of the verb stays the same, despite other modifications.

STEM — The stem is obtained by dropping the final **-en** from the infinitive form (or with a few verbs like **tun** and **ändern** by dropping the final **-n**).

MODIFICATIONS — The various principal parts are formed by adding various prefixes and/or suffixes to the stem (see *What are Prefixes and Suffixes?*, p. 31).

- the past tense is formed by adding a **-t-** (or **-et-** if the verb stem ends in **-d** or **-t**) to the stem of the infinitive + the endings for the different persons.
- the past participle is usually formed by adding the prefix **ge-** and the suffix **-t** or **-et** to the stem of the infinitive.

INFINITIVE	PAST TENSE (3rd per. sing.)	PAST PARTICIPLE
to make	mach**en**	mach**te**	ge**macht**
to work	arbeit**en**	arbeit**ete**	ge**arbeitet**

IRREGULAR VERBS ALSO KNOWN AS "STRONG VERBS"

Strong verbs resemble English irregular verbs in that they have unpredictable principal parts. The irregularity of strong verbs is shown in a variety of ways.

- the vowel of the verb stem often changes in the past tense and in the past participle.
- the past tense endings are different than those for weak verbs.
- the past participle is usually formed by adding the prefix **ge-** and the ending **-en** or **-n**.

	1ST INFINITIVE	2ND PAST TENSE	3RD PAST PARTICIPLE
to find	finden	fand	gefunden
to come	kommen	kam	gekommen
to do	tun	tat	getan

Besides the irregularities listed above, other verbs show their irregularity in different ways:

- **Stem-changing verbs,** so called because in addition to the irregularities listed above the stem vowel of the infinitive changes in the present tense. For these verbs you will need to know a fourth principal part, the 3rd person singular of the present tense.

	1ST INFINITIVE	2ND PAST TENSE	3RD PAST PARTICIPLE	4TH PRESENT TENSE
to run	laufen	lief	gelaufen	läuft
to read	lesen	las	gelesen	liest
to take	nehmen	nahm	genommen	nimmt

- **Mixed-verbs,** so-called because some forms of the verb follow the regular pattern and some forms are irregular. Your German textbook will show you how to form the principal parts of these verbs.

PREFIXES (see p. 33)

Weak and strong verbs with an inseparable prefix do not add the prefix **ge-**. Verbs with separable prefixes add **–ge-** between the prefix and the stem.

INSEPARABLE	be**such**en	be**such**te	be**such**t	*to visit*
SEPARABLE	**aus**suchen	suchte...aus	aus**ge**sucht	*to choose*
INSEPARABLE	be**kommen**	bekam	bekommen	*to receive*
SEPARABLE	**mit**kommen	kam...mit	mit**ge**kommen	*to come along*

Most German dictionaries include an alphabetized list of irregular verbs with their principal parts. By memorizing the principal parts of verbs you will be able conjugate verbs properly in all their tenses.

STUDY TIPS — PRINCIPAL PARTS OF VERBS

Pattern

When you learn a new strong verb, look for another strong verb that changes its vowels in the past tense and the past participle in the same way. Make your own lists of strong verbs according to the vowel pattern in the principal parts.

INFINITIVE	PAST TENSE	PAST PARTICIPLE
-ei-	**-ie-**	**-ie-**
schreiben *(to write)*	schrieb	geschrieben
bleiben *(to stay)*	blieb	geblieben
-i-	**-a-**	**-u-**
finden *(to find)*	fand	gefunden
trinken *(to drink)*	trank	getrunken
-ie-	**-o-**	**-o-**
fliegen *(to fly)*	flog	geflogen
verlieren *(to lose)*	verlor	verloren

Flashcard

1. To review the principal parts of verbs, take out the flashcards you created to learn the meaning of verbs (see p. 51) and sort them into two
groups: weak verbs and strong verbs. On the German side, write
weak or strong and add the principal parts: infinitive, past, past participle.

(weak)	kaufen	kaufte	gekauft
(strong)	gehen	ging	gegangen

2. Work with your flashcards in two ways:

   a. Group the strong verbs according to the vowel patterns you
   determined above. Practice saying the pattern out loud for each
   verb in the group. Repeat the pattern until you can remember it
   without looking at the card.

   b. Mix the strong and weak verbs together and go through the
   cards. As you practice forming the past participle, keep the following in mind:
   Identify if the verb is weak or strong.
   - if weak, you need –t in the past participle.
   - if strong, you need -en in the past participle.
   - if strong, focus on the vowel pattern.
   - if there is a prefix, determine if it is separable or inseparable.
   - if separable, insert –ge- between the prefix and the stem.
   - if inseparable, no ge- is used.

CHAPTER

35

WHAT IS THE PAST TENSE?

The PAST TENSE is used to express an action that occurred in
the past.

> I *saw* you yesterday.

IN ENGLISH

There are several verb forms that indicate the past tense

I worked	SIMPLE PAST
I was working	PAST PROGRESSIVE
I used to work	WITH HELPING VERB USED TO
I did work	PAST EMPHATIC
I have worked	PRESENT PERFECT
I had worked	PAST PERFECT

The simple past is a simple tense; that is, it consists of one
word, *worked* in the example above. The other past tenses
are compound tenses; that is, they consist of more than
one word, an auxiliary plus a main verb, *was working, did
work* in the example above (see *What is an Auxiliary Verb?*,
p. 105).

Simple past — There are two ways to form the simple past.
If the verb is regular, the ending *–ed* (or *-d*) is added. If the
verb is irregular, vowel and/or consonant changes are
common.

REGULAR		IRREGULAR	
work	work*ed*	sing	s*a*ng
live	live*d*	see	s*a*w

Present perfect — The present perfect is formed with the
auxiliary *to have* in the present tense + the past participle
of the main verb (see *What is the Present Tense?*, p. 104 and
What is a Participle?, p. 116).

> I *have worked*.
> | |
> present   past participle
>   of *to work*

> I *have seen* that film.
> | |
> present   past participle
>   of *to see*

IN GERMAN

There are two tenses most commonly used for expressing an action in the past: the simple past and the present perfect.

Simple past — The simple past, also called the IMPERFECT (**Imperfekt**) or the PRETERITE (**Präteritum**), consists of only one word: the verb stem + the simple past ending.

> Ich **wohnte** in Hannover.
> |
> verb stem **wohn-** + ending **-te**
> *I **lived** in Hanover. [I **have lived** in Hanover.]*

> Ich **schwamm** jeden Tag.
> |
> verb stem **schwamm-** + no ending
> *I **swam** every day. [I **have swum** every day.]*

The formation of the simple past depends on whether the verb is a strong or a weak verb (see pp. 110-1). Both the spelling of the verb stem and the endings may be affected. Your German textbook will explain in detail the formation of the simple past.

Present perfect — The present perfect tense (**Perfekt**) is a compound tense, consisting of two parts: the auxiliary verbs **haben** *(to have)* or **sein** *(to be)* conjugated in the present tense + the past participle of the main verb. You must memorize which verbs require **haben** and which require **sein** as the auxiliary.

> Ich **habe** in Hannover **gewohnt.**
> | |
> auxiliary **haben** in   past participle of
> present tense   main verb **wohnen**
> *I **have lived** in Hanover. [I **lived** in Hanover.]*

> Ich **bin** jeden Tag **geschwommen.**
> | |
> auxiliary **sein** in   past participle of
> present tense   main verb **schwimmen**
> *I **have swum** every day. [I **swam** every day.]*

CAREFUL — The simple past and the present perfect have equivalent meanings in German. Their difference is one of style and usage: generally, the simple past is used in written German and the perfect in spoken German.

Pattern

Compare the conjugation of weak and strong verbs in the present and the past tense.

WEAK VERB

PRESENT		PAST	
wohnen *(to live)*			
wohne	wohnen	wohnte	wohnten
wohnst	wohnt	wohntest	wohntet
wohnt	wohnen	wohnte	wohnten

STRONG VERB

PRESENT		PAST	
fahren – *(to drive)*			
fahre	fahren	fuhr	fuhren
fährst	fahrt	fuhrst	fuhrt
fährt	fahren	fuhr	fuhren

What similarities and differences do you see?

Endings:
- all verbs and tenses: 1st and 3rd pers. pl. are the same.
- strong and weak verbs past tense: 1st and 3rd pers. sing. are the same.
- strong verbs past tense: 1st and 3rd pers. sing. no ending; other endings same as in present tense.
- weak verbs past tense: all forms insert a -t- or -te- before the ending.

Vowel change:
- weak verbs: no vowel change from present to past.
- strong verbs: stem vowel change in present tense occurs only in the 2nd and 3rd pers. sing.
- strong verbs: stem vowel change in past tense occurs in all forms.

CHAPTER

WHAT IS A PARTICIPLE?

A **PARTICIPLE** is a form of a verb that can be used in one of two ways: with an auxiliary verb to indicate certain tenses or as an adjective to describe something.

> He *has closed* the door.
>
> auxiliary + participle → past tense
>
> He heard me through the *closed* door.
>
> participle describing *door* → adjective

There are two types of participles: the present participle and the past participle.

PRESENT PARTICIPLE
IN ENGLISH

The present participle is easy to recognize because it is the *-ing* form of the verb: *working, studying, dancing, playing.*

The present participle has three primary uses:

- as the main verb in compound tenses with the auxiliary verb *to be* (see *What is an Auxiliary Verb?*, p. 105)

> She *is writing* with her new pen.
>
> present progressive of *to write*
>
> They *were sleeping*.
>
> past progressive of *to sleep*

- as an adjective (see *What is a Descriptive Adjective?*, p. 131)

> The pen is a *writing* instrument.
>
> describes the noun *instrument*
>
> He woke the *sleeping* child.
>
> describes the noun *child*

- in a phrase (see p. 89)

> *Turning the corner*, Tony ran into a tree.
>
> participial phrase describing *Tony*

IN GERMAN

The present participle is always formed by adding -**d** to the infinitive (see *What is an Infinitive?*, p. 29).

INFINITIVE	PRESENT PARTICIPLE
singen	singen**d**
spielen	spielen**d**
sprechen	sprechen**d**

The present participle occurs less frequently in German than in English and it is not used in the same way. However, it is often used as an adjective that takes adjective endings.

> die **singenden** Kinder
> *the **singing** children*

> ein **spielendes** Mädchen
> *a **playing** girl*

CAREFUL — Never assume that an English word ending with -*ing* is translated by its German counterpart ending in -**d**. Keep in mind that English tenses formed with an auxiliary + present participle (she *is singing*, they *were dancing*) do not exist in German. These tenses are expressed by a one word German verb whose tense corresponds to the tense of the auxiliary.

> She *is singing*.
> |
>   present
> Sie **singt**.
> |
>   present

> They *were dancing*.
> |
>   simple past
> Sie **tanzten**.
> |
>   simple past

PRESENT PARTICIPLE VERSUS GERUND

A **VERBAL NOUN**, also called a **GERUND**, is the form of a verb that functions as a noun in a sentence: it can be a subject, a direct object, an indirect object, or an object of a preposition.

It is important that you learn to distinguish an English participle from a gerund since German gerunds differ in form from present participles.

IN ENGLISH

Gerund — A word ending in -*ing* is a gerund if you can use the interrogative pronoun *what* to replace it in a question. The gerund will answer this question.

> *Reading* can be fun.
>> *What* can be fun? Reading.
>> *Reading*, a noun derived from the verb *to read*, is the subject of the sentence.

> We have often thought about *moving*.
>> We often thought about *what*? Moving.
>> *Moving*, a noun derived from the verb *to move*, is the object of the preposition *about*.

Present participle — A word ending in -*ing* is a present participle if you must use the verb *to do* to replace it in a question. The present participle will answer this question.

> We are *reading*.
>> What *are we doing*? Reading.
>> *Reading*, the present participle of the verb *to read*, is part of the compound verb tense.

> The family is *moving* next week.
>> What *is the family doing*? Moving.
>> *Moving*, the present participle of the verb *to move*, is part of the compound verb tense.

IN GERMAN

Gerunds are usually expressed by a neuter noun made from the infinitive of the verb.

>> lesen → **das** Lesen   *to read, reading*
>> singen → **das** Singen   *to sing, singing*

As you can see in the examples below, knowing how to distinguish a gerund from a present participle will enable you to select the correct form for German.

> ***Talking*** *is silver,* ***being silent*** *is gold.* ["Silence is golden."]
>> *What* is silver? Talking.
>> *What* is gold? Being silent.
>> *Talking* and *being silent* are gerunds.

> **Reden** ist Silber, **Schweigen** ist Gold.
> gerund verb   gerund verb

> We ***are talking*** *a lot.*
>> *What are we doing*? Talking.
>> *Talking* is a present participle used in the present tense.

> Wir **reden** viel.
>   verb

PAST PARTICIPLE
IN ENGLISH

The past participle is formed differently, depending on whether the verb is regular or irregular (see p. 109). It is the form of the verb that follows the various forms of the auxiliary *to have*: I *have spoken,* he *has written,* we *have walked.*

The past participle has three primary uses:

- as the main verb in perfect tenses with the auxiliary verb *to have* (see *What is the Past Tense?,* p. 113; *What is the Future Perfect Tense?,* p. 125; and *What is the Past Perfect Tense?,* p. 121)

    I *have written* all that I have to say.

    present perfect of *to write*

    He *had*n't *spoken* to me all day.

    past perfect of *to speak*

- as the main verb in passive voice with the auxiliary verb *to be* (see *What is Meant by Active and Passive Voice?,* p. 162)

    That book *was written* last year.

    past passive

    That language *is* no longer *spoken.*

    present passive

- as an adjective (see *What is a Descriptive Adjective?,* p. 131)

    Is the *written* word more important than the *spoken* word?

    describes the noun *word*   describes the noun *word*

IN GERMAN

The past participle is formed differently depending on whether the verb is weak or strong (see p. 110-1). While most weak verbs form their past participle according to the same rule, strong verbs have irregular past participles that must be memorized.

Weak verbs — The past participles of weak verbs are formed by adding the prefix **ge-** and the suffix **-t** to the stem of the infinitive (see *What is the Infinitive?,* p. 29).

Infinitive	Stem	Past participle	
machen	mach-	**ge**mach**t**	*made*
glauben	glaub-	**ge**glaub**t**	*believed*

120
130
140
150
160

Strong verbs — The past participles of strong verbs often change the stem vowel, and occasionally some of the consonants. The prefix **ge-** and the ending **-en** or **-n** are usually added to the stem.

INFINITIVE	PAST PARTICIPLE	
schlafen	**ge**schlafen	*slept*
gehen	**gegangen**	*gone*
finden	**gefunden**	*found*
liegen	**gelegen**	*lain*

For both strong and weak verbs that already begin with a prefix, there are special rules for forming the past participle (see p. 111 in *What are the Principal Parts of the Verb?*).

As in English, the past participle can be used in the perfect tenses, in the passive, and as an adjective.

- as the main verb in the perfect tenses: **haben** *(to have)* or **sein** *(to be)* + the past participle

> Ich **habe** das Buch **gelesen**.
> *I **have read** the book.*
> *I **read** the book.*

> Ich **bin** nach Hause **gekommen**.
> *I **have come** home.*
> *I **came** home.*

- as the main verb in the passive voice: **werden** *(to become)* + the past participle (see *What is Meant by Active and Passive Voice?*, p. 162)

> Das Buch **wird** von vielen Studenten **gelesen**.
> *The book **is read** by many students.*

- as an adjective with adjective endings (see *What is a Descriptive Adjective?*, p. 131)

> Ich lese den **getippten** Brief.
> *I read the **typed** letter.*

Since there is no way to predict the past participle of a strong verb, you will have to memorize it when you learn the verb (see Study Tips, p. 111).

WHAT IS THE PAST PERFECT TENSE?

The **PAST PERFECT TENSE,** also called the **PLUPERFECT,** is used to express an action completed in the past before another action or event that also occurred in the past.

> They *had* already *gone* by the time I arrived.
>
>   past perfect   simple past
>   1   2
>
> Both actions 1 and 2 occurred in the past, but action 1 preceded action 2. Therefore, action 1 is in the past perfect.

IN ENGLISH

The past perfect is formed with the auxiliary *had* + the past participle of the main verb: *I had walked, he had seen,* etc. (see p. 119 in *What is a Participle?*). In conversation, *had* is often shortened to *'d*.

Don't forget that verb tenses indicate the time that an action occurs. Therefore, when verbs in the same sentence are in the same tense, the actions took place at the same time. In order to show that actions took place at different times, different tenses must be used.

Look at the following examples.

> The mother *was crying* because her son *was leaving*.
>
>   past progressive   past progressive
>   1   1
>
> Action 1 and action 2 took place at the same time.

> The mother *was crying* because her son *had left*.
>
>   past progressive   past perfect
>   1   2
>
> Action 2 took place before action 1.

IN GERMAN

The past perfect, **PLUSQUAMPERFEKT** in German, is formed with the auxiliary verb **haben** *(to have)* or **sein** *(to be)* in the simple past tense + past participle of the main verb (see *What is the Past Tense?*, p. 113).

> Wir **waren** schon ins Kino **gegangen**.
>
> simple past of **sein** *(to be)*   past participle of **gehen** *(to go)*
> *We **had** already **gone** to the movies.*

Wir **hatten** den Film schon **gesehen**.

simple past of **haben** *(to have)*   past participle of **sehen** *(to see)*

*We **had** already **seen** the film.*

Note the order of the verb parts: in the 2nd position the conjugated past tense of the auxiliary and at the end of the sentence the past participle of the main verb.

Generally, the German past perfect is used the same way as the past perfect in English: to express an action or condition that ended before some other past action or condition that may or may not be stated. Notice how we can express the sequence of events by using different tenses.

Verb tense:	Past Perfect -2	Perfect or Simple past -1	Present 0
Time action takes place:	before -1	before 0	now

TIME ACTION TAKES PLACE: 0 → now
    - 1 → before 0
    - 2 → before -1

*They **had** already **left** when I **arrived**.*
Sie **waren** schon **abgefahren**, als ich **ankam**.

      past perfect -2   simple past -1

CAREFUL — You cannot always rely on spoken English to determine when to use the past perfect in German. In many cases, English permits the use of the simple past to describe an action that preceded another, if it is clear which action came first.

Anja *forgot* (that) she *saw* that movie.

    simple past   simple past

Anja *forgot* (that) she *had seen* the movie.

    simple past   past perfect

Although the two sentences above mean the same thing, only the sequence of tenses in the second sentence would be correct in German.

Gabi **hat vergessen**, dass sie den Film **gesehen hatte**.

    perfect -1   past perfect -2

Both actions took place some time in the past. In German, the action of point -2 has to be in the past perfect because it took place before the action of point -1.

WHAT IS THE FUTURE TENSE?

The **FUTURE TENSE** indicates that an action will take
place some time in the future.

> I *will return* the book as soon as I can.
> └──┬──┘
>   future

IN ENGLISH

The future tense is formed with the auxiliary *will* or *shall* +
the dictionary form of the main verb. In conversation
shall and *will* are often shortened to *'ll*.

> Johan and Axel *will do* their homework tomorrow.
> *I'll leave* tonight.

An action that will take place in the future can also be
expressed in the present tense with an adverb of future
time or an expression of future time.

> Max *is meeting* Axel *tomorrow*.
> └────┬────┘   └──┬──┘
> present progressive adverb
>
> Johan *goes* to Berlin *next week*.
> │   └────┬────┘
> present   expression of future time

IN GERMAN

The future tense is formed with the auxiliary verb **werden**
(to become) + the infinitive of the main verb. The verb
werden is conjugated to agree with the subject and the
infinitive remains unchanged. The conjugated verb is
placed in the 2nd position and the infinitive is placed at
the end of the sentence.

> Lukas und Max **werden** ihre Hausaufgabe **schreiben.**
>   │   │
>   3rd pers. pl.   infinitive
> *Lukas and Max **will write** their homework.*
>
> Ich **werde** heute abend **ausgehen.**
>   │   │
> 1st pers. sing.   infinitive
> *I **shall go out** tonight.*

As in English, an action that will take place in the future
can also be expressed in the present tense with an adverb
or an expression of future time.

Hans und Lukas **schreiben morgen** ihre Prüfung.

present + adverb of future time

*Hans and Lukas **are writing** their test **tomorrow**.*

Er **fliegt nächstes Jahr** nach Deutschland.

present + expression of future time

*He **is flying** to Germany **next year**.*

CAREFUL — Be sure to use the correct form of **werden** when forming the future tense in German. The verb form **will** comes from the modal verb **wollen** and does not indicate future tense (see Careful, p. 107).

FUTURE OF PROBABILITY

In addition to expressing an action that will take place in the future, the future tense in German can be used to express a probable fact, or what the speaker feels is probably true. This is called the FUTURE OF PROBABILITY.

IN ENGLISH

The idea of probability is expressed in the present tense accompanied with words such as *must, probably, wonder*.

My keys *must* be around here.
My keys are *probably* around here.
I *wonder* if my keys are around here.

IN GERMAN

Unlike English that uses the present tense, the idea of probability in German is usually expressed with the future tense accompanied with words such as **wohl** *(probably)*, **sicher** *(certainly)*, **wahrscheinlich** *(probably)*, and **vielleicht** *(perhaps)*.

Sie **werden** dieses Buch **sicher kennen**.

adverb (**sicher**) + future tense of **kennen** *(to know)*

*You **surely know** this book.*

adverb *(surely)* + present tense of *to know*

WHAT IS THE FUTURE PERFECT TENSE?

The **FUTURE PERFECT TENSE** is used to express an action that will occur before another action in the future or before a specific time in the future.

> By the time we leave, he *will have finished.*
>
>   future event   future perfect
>   2   1
>
> Both actions 1 and 2 will occur at some future time, but action 1 will be completed before action 2 takes place. Therefore, action 1 is in the future perfect tense.

> I won't meet him. I *will have left* before he arrives.
>
>   future perfect   future event
>   1   2
>
> Both action 1 and event 2 will occur at some future time, but action 1 will be completed before a specific event in the future. Therefore, action 1 is in the future perfect tense.

IN ENGLISH

The future perfect is formed with the auxiliary *will have* + the past participle of the main verb: *I will have walked, she will have gone.* In conversation *will* is often shortened to *'ll.*

The future perfect is often used following expressions such as *by then, by that time, by* + a date.

> By the end of the month, he*'ll have graduated.*
> By June, I*'ll have saved* enough to buy a car.

IN GERMAN

The future perfect in German is formed with the auxiliary **haben** *(to have)* or **sein** *(to be)* in the future tense + past participle of the main verb.

> Wir **werden** den Film **gesehen haben**.
>
>   past participle of **sehen** *(to see)*
>   future tense of **haben** *(to have)*
>
> *We **will have seen** the film.*

Note the order of the verb parts: the conjugated future auxiliary in the 2nd position and, grouped together at the end of the sentence, the past participle of the main verb + its auxiliary in the infinitive.

Generally, the German future perfect is used the same way as the future perfect in English: to express an action that will be completed in the future before some other future action or event, which may or may not be stated. Notice how we can express the sequence of events by using different tenses.

Verb tense:	Present	Future perfect	Future
	0	1	2
Time action takes place:	now	after 0 before 2	after 0 and after 1

TIME ACTION TAKES PLACE:

$0 \rightarrow$ now

$1 \rightarrow$ after 0 and before 2

$2 \rightarrow$ after 0

*They **will have left** before I arrive.*

Sie **werden abgefahren sein**, bevor ich ankomme.

future perfect	event in the future
1	2

Both actions will take place some time in the future. In German, the action of point 1 has to be in the future perfect because it will take place before the event of point 2.

WHAT IS A CONJUNCTION?

A **CONJUNCTION** is a word that links two or more words or groups of words.

> He had to choose between good *and* evil.
>   conjunction

> They left *because* they were bored.
>   conjunction

IN ENGLISH

There are two kinds of conjunctions: coordinating and subordinating.

Coordinating conjunction — joins words, phrases (groups of words without a verb), and clauses (groups of words with a verb) that are equal; it *coordinates* elements of equal rank. The major coordinating conjunctions are *and, but, or, nor, for,* and *yet.*

> good *or* evil
> word   word
>
> over the river *and* through the woods
>   phrase   phrase
>
> They invited us *but* we couldn't go.
>   clause   clause

In the last example, each of the two clauses, "they invited us" and "we couldn't go," expresses a complete thought; each clause is, therefore, a complete sentence that could stand alone. When a clause expresses a complete sentence it is called a **MAIN CLAUSE**. In the above sentence, the coordinating conjunction *but* links two main clauses (see p. 91 in *What is a Sentence?*).

Subordinating conjunction — joins a main clause to a dependent clause; it *subordinates* one clause to another. A **DEPENDENT CLAUSE** does not express a complete thought; it is, therefore, not a complete sentence. A clause introduced by a subordinating conjunction is called a **SUBORDINATE CLAUSE**. Typical subordinating conjunctions are *before, after, since, although, because, if, unless, so that, while, that,* and *when.*

subordinate clause   main clause

Although we were invited, we didn't go.

subordinating
conjunction

main clause   subordinate clause

They left *because* they were bored.

subordinating
conjunction

main clause   subordinate clause

He said *that* he was tired.

subordinating
conjunction

In the above examples, "although we were invited," "because they were bored," and "that he was tired," are all subordinate clauses. They are not complete sentences and each is introduced by a subordinating conjunction.

Notice that the subordinate clause may come either at the beginning of the sentence or after the main clause.

IN GERMAN

As in English, German has coordinating and subordinating conjunctions. Like adverbs and prepositions, conjunctions never change their form.

The major coordinating conjunctions are **und** *(and)*, **oder** *(or)*, **aber** *(but)*, and **denn** *(for)*. Typical subordinating conjunctions include **als** *(when)*, **weil** *(because)*, **wenn** *(if, whenever)*, **dass** *(that)*, **bevor** *(before)*, **während** *(while)*, and **nachdem** *(after)*.

As in English, the subordinate clause may come before or after the main clause. Unlike English where the word order does not change, in German subordinating conjunctions affect word order in the subordinate clause and the main clause.

- in the subordinate clause the conjugated verb is always placed at the end of the clause.

subordinate clause

Ich esse einen Apfel, **weil** ich Hunger **habe**.

subordinating conjunction   verb at end of the subordinate clause
*I'm eating an apple, **because** I am hungry.*

- if the subordinate clause comes at the beginning of the sentence, it functions as the first element in the sen-

tence and the conjugated verb of the main clause is
placed in the 2nd position, right after the conjugated
verb of the subordinate clause, separated by a comma.

subordinate clause 1st position   main clause

Weil ich Hunger **habe**, **esse** ich einen Apfel.

conjugated verb conjugated verb
2nd position

Because I'm hungry, I'm eating an apple.

PREPOSITION OR CONJUNCTION?
IN ENGLISH

Some words function as both prepositions and subordinating conjunctions, for example, *before* and *after*. We can
identify the word's function by determining whether or
not it introduces a clause.

- if the word in question introduces a clause, i.e., a group
  of words with a verb, it is a subordinating conjunction.

  We left *before* the intermission began.

  subordinating   subject + verb → clause
  conjunction

  After the concert was over, we ate ice cream.

  subordinating   subject + verb → clause
  conjunction

- if the word in question is followed by an object, but no
  verb, it is a preposition.

  We left *before* the intermission.

  preposition   object of preposition

  After the concert we ate ice cream.

  preposition object of preposition

IN GERMAN

It is important for you to establish whether a word is a
preposition or a conjunction because in German you will
use different words and apply different rules of grammar
depending on the part of speech.

| English | German | |
PREPOSITION AND CONJUNCTION	PREPOSITION	CONJUNCTION
before	vor	bevor
after	nach	nachdem

Let us look at some examples using these different parts of speech.

- *before* and *after* as conjunctions → **bevor** and **nachdem** connect two clauses and require two parts of speech, i.e., a subject and a verb.

    *We left **before** the intermission began.*

                    subject + verb
    Wir sind weggegangen, **bevor** die Pause anfing.

    After the concert was over, we ate ice cream.

            subject + verb
    Nachdem das Konzert vorbei war, aßen wir Eis.

- *before* and *after* as prepositions → **vor** and **nach** are part of a phrase and require one part of speech, i.e., an object.

    *We left **before** the intermission.*

                    object
    Wir sind **vor** der Pause weggegangen.

    After the concert we ate ice cream.

            object
    Nach dem Konzert haben wir Eis gegessen.

Knowing the part of speech of the new words that you learn will help you choose the correct word in German and apply the proper rules of grammar.

STUDY TIPS — CONJUNCTIONS

Flashcard

1. Make a flashcard for each conjunction. On the English side, write the meaning of the conjunction. On the German side, write "coordinating" or "subordinating" and a sample sentence from your textbook.

2. Sort the flashcards into two categories: coordinating and subordinating. To remember the five cards in the coordinating pile: **sondern, oder, denn, aber, und**, use the acronym **SODAund**. All the other conjunctions belong in the subordinating category.

CHAPTER

41

WHAT IS A DESCRIPTIVE ADJECTIVE?

A **DESCRIPTIVE ADJECTIVE** is a word that indicates a quality of a
noun or pronoun. As the name implies, it *describes* the noun
or pronoun.

> The book is *interesting.*
> noun   descriptive
> described   adjective

IN ENGLISH

A descriptive adjective does not change form, regardless of
the noun or pronoun it modifies.

> The students are *intelligent.*
> She is an *intelligent* person.
>> The form of the adjective *intelligent* remains the same
>> although the persons described are different in number
>> (*students* is plural and *person* is singular).

Descriptive adjectives are divided into two groups depending on how they are connected to the noun they modify.

Predicate adjectives — Predicate adjectives are connected
to the noun they describe, always the subject of the sentence, by **LINKING VERBS** such as *to be, to feel, to look.* (See
What is a Predicate Noun?, p. 44.)

> The children are *good.*
> noun   linking   predicate
> described   verb   adjective

> The house looks *small.*
> noun   linking   predicate
> described   verb   adjective

Attributive adjectives — Attributive adjectives are connected directly to the noun they describe and always precedes it.

> The *good* children were praised.
> attributive   noun
> adjective   described

> The family lives in a *small* house.
> attributive   noun
> adjective   described

IN GERMAN

As in English, descriptive adjectives can be identified as predicate or attributive adjectives according to the way they are connected to the noun they describe. While predicate adjectives do not take special endings in German, attributive adjectives do.

Predicate adjectives — Predicate adjectives have the same form as the dictionary entry for the adjective, regardless of the gender and number of the nouns or pronouns they modify.

> *The chairs are **small**.*
> Die Stühle sind **klein**.
> |
> masculine plural

> *The house is **small**.*
> Das Haus ist **klein**.
> |
> neuter singular

Attributive adjectives — There are three different sets of endings for attributive adjectives: WEAK ENDINGS, STRONG ENDINGS, and MIXED ENDINGS. The type of ending chosen depends on what is needed to indicate the gender, case, and number of the noun described.

To select the appropriate endings in your textbook, follow these steps:

1. NOUN DESCRIBED — Identify the noun described by the attributive adjective.
2. ENDING OF ATTRIBUTIVE ADJECTIVE — Look if the word preceding the noun described reveals the noun's gender, case, and number.

   - weak ending — when the noun is preceded by a **der**-word, such as a definite article, the gender, case, and number is indicated by the **der**-word. These are the most common adjective endings: **der** gelb**e** Fisch, **die** bunt**en** Autos.

   - strong ending — when the noun described is not preceded by an article, the gender, case, and number are indicated on the adjective instead: gelb**er** Fisch, blau**es** Auto.

   - mixed ending — when the noun is preceded by an **ein**-word, such as an indefinite article, some have strong endings (nominative and accusative singular) and the others have weak endings: **ein** gelb**er** Fisch, **einem** gelb**en** Fisch.

To show you the variety of possible endings, below are the three sets of endings of attributive adjectives in the nominative case: **Fisch** *(fish)*, masculine; **Blume** *(flower)*, feminine; **Auto** *(car)* neuter.

AFTER DER-WORD	AFTER EIN-WORD	NO ARTICLE
der gelbe Fisch	ein gelber Fisch	gelber Fisch
the yellow fish	*a yellow fish*	*yellow fish*
die rote Blume	eine rote Blume	rote Blume
the red flower	*a red flower*	*red flower*
das blaue Auto	ein blaues Auto	blaues Auto
the blue car	*a blue car*	*blue car*
die bunten Autos	keine bunten Autos	bunte Autos
the colorful car	*no colorful cars*	*colorful cars*

90

Your textbook will give you charts of the various endings for attributive adjectives.

STUDY TIPS — DESCRIPTIVE ADJECTIVES

Pattern
Compare the pattern of the 3 types of endings of attributive adjectives.

DER-WORDS (weak endings)

	MASC.	FEM.	NEUT.	PL.
NOM.	der gelbe Fisch	die rote Blume	das blaue Auto	die bunten Autos
ACC.	den gelben Fisch	die rote Blume	das blaue Auto	die bunten Autos
DAT.	dem gelben Fisch	der roten Blume	dem blauen Auto	den bunten Autos
GEN.	des gelben Fisches	der roten Blume	des blauen Autos	der bunten Autos

What patterns do you see?
■ endings → -e or **-en**
■ nom. sing. endings → **-e**
■ acc. sing. endings: fem. and neut. → **-e**; masc. → **-en**
■ dative, genitive, and plural endings → **-en**

NO ARTICLE (strong endings)

	MASC.	FEM.	NEUT.	PL.
NOM.	gelber Fisch	rote Blume	blaues Auto	bunte Autos
ACC.	gelben Fisch	rote Blume	blaues Auto	bunte Autos
DAT.	gelbem Fisch	roter Blume	blauem Auto	bunten Autos
GEN.	gelbes Fisches	roter Blume	blaues Autos	bunter Autos

What pattern do you see?
■ endings → same as definite articles (see above and p. 39).

EIN-WORDS (mixed endings)

	MASC.	FEM.	NEUT.	PL.
NOM.	ein gelber Fisch	eine rote Blume	ein blaues Auto	keine bunten Autos
ACC.	einen gelben Fisch	eine rote Blume	ein blaues Auto	keine bunten Autos
DAT.	einem gelben Fisch	einer roten Blume	einem blauen Auto	keinen bunten Autos
GEN.	eines gelben Fisches	einer roten Blume	eines blauen Autos	keiner bunten Autos

What patterns do you see?

- nom. and acc. sing. strong endings → same as definite articles
- dat., gen., and pl. weak endings → **–en**

Practice

1. Create a list of common adjectives.
2. Write sentences using those adjectives as attributive adjectives with both **der**-words and **ein**-words to describe masc., fem., neut. sing. and pl. nouns functioning as subjects, indirect, and direct objects.

Subject → nominative case

> **Der junge Mann** geht ins Restaurant.
> *The young man goes to the restaurant.*

> **Ein junger Mann** geht ins Restaurant.
> *A young man goes to the restaurant.*

Direct object → accusative case

> Die Frau sieht **den jungen Mann**.
> *The woman sees **the young man**.*

> Die Frau sieht **einen jungen Mann**.
> *The woman sees **a young man**.*

Indirect object → dative case

> Die Frau gibt **dem jungen Mann** die Karte.
> *The woman gives **the young man** the menu.*

> Die Frau gibt **einem jungen Mann** die Karte.
> *The woman gives **a young man** the menu.*

Possessor → genitive case

> Der Hund **des jungen Mannes** sitzt neben ihm.
> *The young man's dog sits beside him.*

> Der Hund **eines jungen Mannes** sitzt neben ihm.
> *A young man's dog sits beside him*

WHAT IS MEANT BY COMPARISON
OF ADJECTIVES?

The term COMPARISON OF ADJECTIVES is used when two or more   1
persons or things have the same quality (height, size, color,
any characteristic) indicated by a descriptive adjective and
we want to show which of these persons or things has a
greater, lesser, or equal degree of that quality.

> comparison of adjectives
> Hansel is *tall* but Gretel is *taller*.
>
> adjective   adjective
> modifies *Hansel*   modifies *Gretel*

> Both nouns, *Hansel* and *Gretel*, have the same quality indicated by   10
> the adjective *tall,* and we want to show that Gretel has a greater
> degree of that quality (i.e., she is *taller* than Hansel).

In English and in German, there are two types of comparison: comparative and superlative.

COMPARATIVE

The comparative compares a quality of a person or thing
with the same quality in another person or thing. The comparison can indicate that one or the other has more, less, or
the same amount of that quality.
                                                                  20
IN ENGLISH

Let's go over the three degrees of comparison.

The comparative of GREATER DEGREE (more) is formed differently depending on the length of the adjective being com-
pared.

- short adjective + *-er* + *than*
  Gretel is tall*er* *than* Hansel.
  Ingrid is young*er* *than* her sister.

- *more* + longer adjective + *than*
  Axel is *more* intelligent *than* Franz.   30
  His car is *more* expensive *than* ours.

The comparitive of LESSER DEGREE (less) is formed as fol-
lows: *not as* + adjective + *as*, or *less* + adjective + *than*.
  Hansel is *not as* tall *as* Gretel.
  My car is *less* expensive *than* your car.

The comparitive of **EQUAL DEGREE** (same) is formed as follows: *as* + adjective + *as*.

> Axel is *as* tall *as* Franz.
>
> My car is *as* expensive *as* his car.

IN GERMAN

As in English, the comparative has the same three degrees of comparison of adjectives. Unlike English, the structure used does not depend on the length of the adjective.

The comparative of **GREATER DEGREE** is formed by adding an umlaut to the stem vowels **a**, **o**, and **u** + **-er** to the stem of the adjective. The structure and the ending is different for predicate and attributive adjectives (see p.132).

- **predicate adjective** — The comparative is the two-word form: (adjective + umlaut + **-er**) + **als** *(than)*.

> Ingrid ist j**ün**ger **als** ihr Bruder.
>
> predicate adjective + umlaut + **-er** + **als**
> *Ingrid is younger **than** her brother.*

> Das Buch ist interessant**er als** der Film.
>
> predicate adjective + **-er** + **als**
> *The book is **more** interesting **than** the film.*

- **attributive adjective** — The comparative is the one-word form: adjective + umlaut + **-er-** + adjective ending, i.e., weak, strong, or mixed.

> Ich kenne das j**ün**g**ere** Mädchen nicht.
>
> attributive adjective + umlaut + **-er-** + weak ending
> *I don't know the younger girl.*

> Das ist ein interessant**erer** Film.
>
> attributive adjective + **-er-** + strong ending
> *That is a **more** interesting film.*

CAREFUL — Do not confuse the regular –er adjective ending with the comparative –er ending.

REGULAR ADJECTIVE	COMPARATIVE ADJECTIVE
ein **bunter** Garten	ein bunt**erer** Garten
a colorful garden	*a **more** colorful garden*
ein **kleiner** Hund	ein klein**erer** Hund
a small dog	*a smaller dog*

The comparative of **LESSER DEGREE** is formed as follows: **nicht so** *(less)* + adjective + **wie** *(than)*.

Tina ist **nicht so gross wie** Franz.
*Tina is **not as tall as** Franz.*

Tina ist **nicht so jung wie** Ingrid.
*Tina is **not as young as** Ingrid.*

The comparitive of **EQUAL DEGREE** is formed as follows: **so** *(as)* + adjective + **wie** *(as).*

Axel ist **so gross wie** Anja.
*Axel is **as tall as** Anja.*

Mein Auto ist **so teuer wie** sein Auto.
*My car is **as expensive as** his car.*

SUPERLATIVE

The superlative form is used to stress the highest or lowest degrees of a quality.

IN ENGLISH

Let's go over the two degrees of the superlative.

The superlative of **HIGHEST DEGREE** is formed differently depending on the length of the adjective.

- *the* + short adjective + *-est*

    Ingrid is *the* calm*est* in the family.
    My car is *the* saf*est* on the market.

- *the most* + long adjective

    That argument was *the most* convincing.
    This book is *the most* interesting of all.

The superlative of **LOWEST DEGREE** is formed as follows: *the least* + adjective.

Hans is *the least* active.
Her car is *the least* expensive of all.

IN GERMAN

As in English, there are two degrees of the superlative.

The superlative of **HIGHEST DEGREE** is formed by adding an umlaut to the stem vowels **a, o,** and **u** + **-st** or **-est** to the stem of the adjective. The structure and the ending of the superlative form is different for predicate and attributive adjectives.

- **predicate adjective** — The superlative is the two word form: **am** + (adjective + umlaut + **-st-** or **-est-** + **-en**).

    Dieses Buch ist **am** ältesten.
    *This book is **the** oldest.*

    Inge ist **am** kleinsten.
    *Inge is **the** smallest.*

80

90

100

110

120

- **attributive adjective** — The superlative is the two-word form: definite article + (adjective + umlaut + -st- or -est- + weak adjective ending).

    Hier ist **das älteste** Buch.
    *Here is **the oldest** book.*

    Inge ist **das** kleinste Mädchen in der Schule.
    *Inge is **the smallest** girl in the school.*

¹³⁰ The superlative of **LOWEST DEGREE** is a three-word form: **am wenigsten** + adjective.

    Hans ist **am wenigsten** flexibel.
    *Hans is **the least** flexible.*

    Ihr Auto ist **am wenigsten** teuer.
    *Her car is **the least** expensive.*

CAREFUL — In English and in German there are several adjectives that form the comparative and the superlative in irregular ways.

¹⁴⁰

good	gut	*much*	viel
better	besser	*more*	mehr
best	am besten	*most*	am meisten

You will find a list of irregular comparative and superlative forms in your German textbook that you will have to memorize.

WHAT IS AN ADVERB?

An **ADVERB** is a word that describes a verb, an adjective, or another adverb. It indicates manner, degree, time, place.[1]

> Julia drives *well*.
>   verb adverb

> The house is *very* big.
>   adverb adjective

> The girl ran *too quickly*.
>   adverb adverb

IN ENGLISH

There are different types of adverbs:

- an **ADVERB OF MANNER** answers the question *how?* Adverbs of manner are the most common and they are easy to recognize because they end with *-ly*.

  > Ingrid sings *beautifully*.

  > *Beautifully* describes the verb *sings*; it tells you how Ingrid sings.

- an **ADVERB OF DEGREE** answers the question *how much?*

  > Axel did *well* on the exam.

- an **ADVERB OF TIME** answers the question *when?*

  > He will come *soon*.

- an **ADVERB OF PLACE** answers the question *where?*

  > The children were left *behind*.

A few adverbs in English are identical in form to the corresponding adjectives (see *What is an Adjective?*, p. 75).

ADVERB	ADJECTIVE
The guests came *late*.	We greeted the *late* guests.
Don't drive so *fast*.	*Fast* drivers cause accidents.
She works very *hard*.	This is *hard* work.

CAREFUL — Remember that in English *good* is an adjective since it modifies a noun and *well* is an adverb since it modifies a verb.

---

[1]In English and in German, the structure for comparing adverbs is the same as the structure for comparing predicate adjectives (see *What is Meant by Comparison of Adjectives?*, p. 135).

The student writes *good* English.

> *Good* modifies the noun *English;* it is an adjective.

The student writes *well.*

> *Well* modifies the verb *writes;* it is an adverb.

IN GERMAN

As in English, there are words that function only as adverbs.

> Das Haus ist **sehr** groß.
> *The house is **very** big.*
>
> Er kommt **bald**.
> *He is coming **soon**.*

In German however, many adverbs, particularly adverbs of manner, have the same form as their corresponding adjective.

ADVERB	ADJECTIVE
Du hast das **gut** gemacht.	Dieses Buch ist **gut**.
*You did that **well**.*	*This book is **good**.*
Sie singen **schön**.	Das Lied ist **schön**.
*They sing **beautifully**.*	*The song is **beautiful**.*
Wir fahren **schnell**.	Der Wagen ist **schnell**.
*We drive **fast**.*	*The car is **fast**.*

You will have to memorize adverbs as vocabulary items. The most important fact for you to remember is that adverbs are invariable; i.e., they never change form.

CAREFUL — In English, the word order for adverbs is manner + place + time. In German, it is time + manner + place.

> *I am traveling by train to Munich **tomorrow**.*
> | | |
>   manner   place   time
>
> Ich fahre **morgen** mit dem Zug nach München.
> | | |
>   time   manner   place

Consult your textbook for the placement of adverbs.

STUDY TIPS — ADVERBS

Flashcards

Create flashcards for each German adverb you learn and its English equivalent.

früh	*early*
nie	*never*
langsam	*slowly*

WHAT ARE REFLEXIVE PRONOUNS
AND VERBS?

A **REFLEXIVE VERB** is a verb that is accompanied by a pronoun, called a **REFLEXIVE PRONOUN**, that serves *to reflect* the action of the verb back to the subject.

subject   reflexive pronoun → the same person

She *cut herself* with the knife.

reflexive verb

IN ENGLISH

Many verbs can take on a reflexive meaning by adding a reflexive pronoun.

The child *dresses* the doll.

regular verb

The child *dresses herself*.

verb + reflexive pronoun

Reflexive pronouns end with *-self* in the singular and *-selves* in the plural.

	SUBJECT PRONOUN	**REFLEXIVE PRONOUN**
SINGULAR		
1ST PERSON	I	myself
2ND PERSON	you	yourself
3RD PERSON	he	himself
	she	herself
	it	itself
PLURAL		
1ST PERSON	we	ourselves
2ND PERSON	you	yourselves
3RD PERSON	they	themselves

As the subject changes so does the reflexive pronoun, because they both refer to the same person or object.

I cut *myself*.
Hans and Julia blamed *themselves* for the accident.

Although the subject pronoun *you* is the same for the singular and plural, there is a difference in the reflexive pronouns: *yourself* (singular) is used when you are speaking to one person and *yourselves* (plural) is used when you are speaking to more than one.

> *Johan,* did *you* make *yourself* a sandwich?
> *Children,* make sure *you* wash *yourselves* properly.

Reflexive verbs can be in any tense: *I wash myself* (present), *I washed myself* (past), *I will wash myself* (future), etc. Reflexive pronouns can function as either direct objects, indirect objects, or objects of a preposition, but the form is the same regardless of the function (see *What is an Object?,* p. 53 and *What is a Preposition?,* p. 62).

IN GERMAN
REFLEXIVE PRONOUNS

As in English, there is a different reflexive pronoun for each person. Since the reflexive pronoun can function as a direct object, indirect object, or object of a preposition, German reflexive pronouns have an accusative and dative form. As you can see in the chart below, the same form is used for accusative and dative reflexive pronouns, except for the 1st and 2nd persons singular.

SUBJECT	REFLEXIVE		
NOMINATIVE	ACCUSATIVE	DATIVE	
ich	mich	mir	*myself*
du	dich	dir	*yourself*
er			
sie	sich	sich	*himself, herself,*
es			*itself*
wir	uns	uns	*ourselves*
ihr	euch	euch	*yourselves*
sie	sich	sich	*themselves*
Sie	sich	sich	*yourself, yourselves*

Here are a few sentences illustrating the use of the accusative or dative reflexive pronoun, depending on its function, the verb and the preposition.

- as direct or indirect object of the verb

> *I cut **myself** with the knife.*
> |
>   direct object of *cut*

Ich habe **mich** mit dem Messer geschnitten.
      |
  accusative object of **geschnitten** *(to cut)*

*You should write **yourself** a note.*
     |
     indirect object of *write*
     You should write *to whom*? To yourself → indirect object   80
Du solltest **dir** einen Zettel schreiben.
      |
     dative object of **schreiben** *(to write)*

- as object of a preposition
  *He thinks only of **himself**.*
            |
       object of preposition *of*
       to think of → **denken an** + accusative
  Er denkt nur an **sich**.
           |
       accusative object of **denken an**

    90

  *You talk about **yourself** too much.*
          |
       object of preposition *about*
       to talk about → **reden von** + dative
  Du redest zuviel von **dir**.
            |
       dative object of **von**

REFLEXIVE VERBS

Some German verbs are called **REFLEXIVE VERBS** because they must have reflexive pronouns to complete their meaning. The English equivalents of these verbs do not have reflexive pronouns. Reflexive verbs are listed in the dictionary with the 3rd person reflexive pronoun **sich** + the infinitive.

sich erholen	*to recover*
sich befinden	*to be located*
sich verlieben	*to fall in love*

As in English, German reflexive verbs are conjugated in the various persons followed by a reflexive pronoun. Look at the conjugation of **sich erholen** *(to recover)* that takes an accusative object.

    100

    110

SINGULAR

1ST PERSON	ich erhole mich	*I recover*
2ND PERSON FAMILIAR	du erholst dich	*you recover*
	er erholt sich	*he, it recovers*
3RD PERSON	sie erholt sich	*she, it recovers*
	es erholt sich	*it recovers*

PLURAL

1ST PERSON	wir erholen uns	*we recover*
2ND PERSON FAMILIAR	ihr erholt euch	*you recover*
3RD PERSON	sie erholen sich	*they recover*
2ND PERSON FORMAL	Sie erholen sich	*you recover*

    120

As in English, reflexive verbs can be conjugated in all tenses. The subject pronoun and reflexive pronoun remain the same; only the verb form changes: *du* **erholst** *dich* (present), *du* **wirst** *dich* **erholen** (future), *du* **hast** *dich* **erholt** (perfect).

As you learn new vocabulary, you will need to memorize which German verbs require a reflexive pronoun as part of the whole verb. A number of verbs can be used with or without reflexive pronouns, and sometimes verbs have a different meaning when they are reflexive. Your German textbook will introduce you to these verbs.

CAREFUL — Pay special attention to verbs that take a direct object in English but require the dative case in German.

> *I can't help* **myself.**
> |
> direct object of *help*
> Remember: *to help* → **helfen** + dative
> Ich kann **mir** nicht helfen.
> |
> dative object of **helfen**

RECIPROCAL ACTION

IN ENGLISH

English uses a regular verb followed by the expression "each other" to express reciprocal action, that is, an action between two or more persons or things.

> The dog and the cat looked at *each other.*
> > The expression "each other" tells us that the action of *looking* was reciprocal, i.e., the dog looked at the cat and the cat looked at the dog.

> Our children call *each other* every day.
> > The expression "each other" tells us that the action of *calling* is reciprocal, i.e., the various children call one another every day.

Since reciprocal verbs require that more than one person or thing be involved, the verb is always plural.

IN GERMAN

German uses reflexive pronouns to express an action that is reciprocal.

> Wir **sehen uns** morgen.
> *We'll* **see each other** *tomorrow.*

> Unsere Kinder **rufen sich** jeden Tag an.
> *Our children* **call each other** *every day.*

Flashcards

Create flashcards for reflexive verbs. On the German side, include **sich** and the infinitive form of the verb and indicate the case of the reflexive pronoun. Finally, write two sample sentences in the first and third person singular.

sich freuen	*to be happy* about something
(acc.)	**Ich freue mich** über das Wetter.
	I'm happy about the weather.
	Er freut sich über das Wetter.
	He is happy about the weather.

WHAT IS A RELATIVE PRONOUN?

A **RELATIVE PRONOUN** is a word used at the beginning of a clause that gives additional information about someone or something previously mentioned.

clause

additional information about *the book*

I'm reading the book *that* the teacher recommended.

A relative pronoun serves two purposes:

- as a pronoun it stands for a noun previously mentioned. The noun to which it refers is called the **ANTECEDENT**.

Here comes the boy *who* broke the window.

antecedent of the relative pronoun *who*

- it introduces a **SUBORDINATE CLAUSE**; that is, a group of words having a subject and a verb that cannot stand alone because it does not express a complete thought. A subordinate clause is dependent on a **MAIN CLAUSE**; that is, another group of words having a subject and a verb that can stand alone as a complete sentence.

main clause   subordinate clause

Here comes the boy *who broke the window.*

verb   subject verb

A subordinate clause that starts with a relative pronoun is also called a **RELATIVE CLAUSE**. In the example above, the relative clause starts with the relative pronoun *who* and gives us additional information about the antecedent *boy*.

Relative clauses are very common. We use them in everyday speech without giving much thought as to how we construct them. The relative pronoun allows us to combine two thoughts, which have a common element, into a single sentence.

COMBINING SENTENCES WITH A RELATIVE PRONOUN

When sentences are combined with a relative pronoun, the relative pronoun can have different functions in the relative clause. It can be the subject, the direct object, the indirect object, or the object of a preposition.

Let us look at some examples of how sentences are combined.

- relative pronoun as a subject (see p. 41)

  > SENTENCE A The students passed the exam.
  > SENTENCE B They studied.

  1. COMMON ELEMENT — Identify the element the two sentences have in common.

     > Both *the students* and *they* refer to the same persons.

  2. ANTECEDENT — The common element in the first sentence will be the antecedent of the relative pronoun and will remain unchanged. The common element in the second sentence will be replaced by a relative pronoun.

     > *The students* is the antecedent and remains unchanged.
     > *They* will be replaced by a relative pronoun.

  3. FUNCTION — The relative pronoun in the relative clause has the same function as the word it replaces.

     > *They* is the subject of *studied*. Therefore,
     > the relative pronoun will be the subject of *studied*.

  4. PERSON OR THING — Choose the relative pronoun according to whether its antecedent refers to a person or a thing.

     > The antecedent *students* refers to persons.

  5. SELECTION — Select the relative pronoun.

     > *Who* or *that* is the subject relative pronoun
     > referring to a person or persons.

  6. RELATIVE CLAUSE — Place the relative pronoun at the beginning of the second sentence (sentence B), thus forming a relative clause.

     > *who* studied
     > *that* studied

  7. PLACEMENT — To combine the two clauses, place the relative clause right after its antecedent.

     > The students *who* studied passed the exam.
     > The students *that* studied passed the exam.
     > |_____|
     >   antecedent   relative clause

- relative pronoun as a direct object (see p. 53)

  > SENTENCE A This is the student.
  > SENTENCE B I saw him.
  >   1. COMMON ELEMENT: *the student* and *him*
  >   2. ANTECEDENT: the student
  >   3. FUNCTION: *him* is the direct object

4. PERSON OR THING: *the student* is a person
5. SELECTION: *that* or *whom*
6. RELATIVE CLAUSE: *that (whom)* I saw
7. PLACEMENT: the student + *that (whom)* I saw

This is the student *(that)* I saw.
This is the student *(whom)* I saw.

antecedent   relative clause

- relative pronoun as an indirect object (see p. 55)

SENTENCE A   This is the student.
SENTENCE B   I spoke to him.

1. COMMON ELEMENT: *the student* and *him*
2. ANTECEDENT: the student
3. FUNCTION: *him* is the indirect object
4. PERSON OR THING: *the student* is a person
5. SELECTION: *to whom*
6. RELATIVE CLAUSE: *to whom* I spoke
7. PLACEMENT: the student + *to whom* I spoke

This is the student *to whom* I spoke.

antecedent relative clause

- relative pronoun as an object of a preposition (see p. 62)

SENTENCE A   This is the student.
SENTENCE B   I spoke with him.

1. COMMON ELEMENT: *the student* and *him*
2. ANTECEDENT: the student
3. FUNCTION: *him* is the object of the preposition *with*
4. PERSON OR THING: *the student* is a person
5. SELECTION: *whom*
6. RELATIVE CLAUSE: *with whom* I spoke
7. PLACEMENT: the student + *with whom* I spoke

This is the student *with whom* I spoke.

antecedent   relative clause

SELECTION OF THE RELATIVE PRONOUN
IN ENGLISH

The selection of a relative pronoun in English often depends not only on its function in the relative clause, but also on whether its antecedent is a "person" (human beings and animals) or a "thing" (objects and ideas).

In an English sentence, relative pronouns can sometimes be omitted in a sentence.

The book *that* I'm reading is interesting.

relative pronoun
The book I'm reading is interesting.

IN GERMAN

Unlike English, the same set of relative pronouns is used for antecedents referring to persons and things and, moreover, they can never be omitted in a sentence. German relative pronouns are based on two factors:

- their gender and number reflect the gender and number of their antecedent
- their case form reflects their function in the relative   130 clause

We shall look at each function separately. (Notice that relative clauses are always separated by a comma from the main clause.)

SUBJECT OF THE RELATIVE CLAUSE
(see *What is a Subject?*, p. 41)

IN ENGLISH

There are three relative pronouns that can be used as subjects of a relative clause, depending on whether the relative pronoun refers to a person or a thing. When it is the   140 subject of a relative clause, the relative pronoun is never omitted.

Person — *who* or *that* → subject of the relative clause

$$\overbrace{\qquad\qquad\qquad\qquad}^{\text{relative clause}}$$

She is the only student *who* answered all the time.
She is the only student *that* answered all the time.

Thing — *which* or *that* → subject of the relative clause

$$\overbrace{\qquad\qquad}^{\text{relative clause}}$$

The movie *which* is so popular was filmed in Germany.   150
The movie *that* is so popular was filmed in Germany.

antecedent   relative pronoun
                    subject of *is*

Notice that the relative pronoun subject is always followed by a verb.

IN GERMAN

Relative pronouns that are the subject of the relative clause are in the nominative case. The form used depends on the gender and number of the antecedent.

160

Singular		
MASCULINE	der	
FEMININE	die	*who, that, which*
NEUTER	das	
Plural	die	

To choose the correct form,

1. ANTECEDENT — Find the antecedent. (Don't forget that the antecedent is always the noun that precedes the relative pronoun.)
2. NUMBER & GENDER — Determine the number and gender of the antecedent.
3. SELECTION — Select the corresponding form in the nominative case.

Here is an example.

*The man **who** visited us was nice.*
  1. ANTECEDENT: man
  2. NUMBER & GENDER: **der Mann** *(the man)* is masculine singular
  3. SELECTION: masculine singular nominative → **der**

Der Mann, **der** uns besuchte, war nett.

DIRECT AND INDIRECT OBJECTS OF THE RELATIVE CLAUSE
(see *What is an Object?*, p. 53)

IN ENGLISH

There are three relative pronouns that can be used as direct or indirect objects of a relative clause, depending on whether the relative pronoun refers to a person or a thing. Since relative pronouns are often omitted when they are objects of a relative clause, we have indicated them in parentheses in the examples below.

Person — *whom* or *that* → object of a relative clause.

- as a direct object

  relative clause
  This is the student *(whom)* I saw yesterday.

  relative clause
  This is the student *(that)* I saw yesterday.

- as an indirect object

  relative clause
  Ingrid is the person *to whom* he gave the present.

Thing — *which* or *that* → object of a relative clause.

- as a direct object

  relative clause
  This is the book *(which)* Axel bought.
  This is the book *(that)* Axel bought.

- as an indirect object

  relative clause
  Here is the library *to which* he gave the book.

IN GERMAN

Relative pronouns that are the object of the relative clause are either in the accusative or dative case. The form used depends on the gender and number of the antecedent. 210

	ACCUSATIVE	DATIVE	
SINGULAR			
MASCULINE	den	dem	
FEMININE	die	der	*who, that, which*
NEUTER	das	dem	
PLURAL	die	denen	

Unlike English, relative pronouns are never omitted in German. (The equivalent English relative pronouns below are in parentheses for reference.) 220

- as a direct object → accusative

> *Here is the student (**whom**) Franz saw last night.*
> Hier ist der Student, **den** Franz gestern Abend sah.
> | |
>   masc. sing. masc. sing. accusative

> *The bag (**that**) I'm buying is expensive.*
> Die Tasche, **die** ich kaufe, ist teuer.
> | |
>   fem. sing. fem. sing. accusative

- as an indirect object → dative 230

> *Here is the student Franz gave the book **to**.*
>   RESTRUCTURED: *Here is the student **to** whom Franz gave the book.*
> Hier ist der Student, **dem** Franz das Buch gab.
> | |
>   masc. sing.   masc. sing. dative

> *The cat (**that**) the dog followed was black.*
> Die Katze, **der** der Hund folgte, war schwarz.
> | |
>   fem. sing. fem. sing. dative

240

RELATIVE PRONOUN AS OBJECT OF A PREPOSITION
(see p. 62 and pp. 64-5 in *What is a Preposition?*)

IN ENGLISH

Relative pronouns used as objects of a preposition are the same as those used as direct and indirect objects. As is the case with other relative pronouns used as objects, they are often omitted. (We have indicated these relative pronouns in parentheses in the examples below.) By restructuring the English sentence to avoid a dangling preposition, you will restore the relative pronoun. 250

Person — *whom* or *that* → object of a preposition in a relative clause

relative clause

Ingrid is the person *(that)* he went out *with*.

relative pronoun — dangling preposition

Ingrid is the person *with whom* he went out.

preposition + relative pronoun

Thing — *which* or *that* → object of a preposition in a relative clause

relative clause

This is the library *(that)* I was talking *about*.

relative pronoun — dangling preposition

This is the library *about which* I was talking.

preposition + relative pronoun

IN GERMAN

Relative pronouns that are the object of a preposition are in the case required by the preposition and the gender is determined by the antecedent. Since German places prepositions directly preceding their objects, you will need to restructure English phrases with dangling prepositions.

Here is the person I was waiting for.
RESTRUCTURED: *Here is the person for whom I was waiting.*
Hier ist die Person, **auf die** ich wartete.

fem. sing.   fem. sing. **auf** + accusative

Here is the person I was speaking with.
RESTRUCTURED: *Here is the person with whom I was speaking.*
Hier ist die Person, **mit der** ich sprach.

fem. sing.   fem. sing. **mit** + dative

RELATIVE PRONOUN AS POSSESSIVE MODIFIER "WHOSE"

IN ENGLISH

The possessive modifier *whose* does not change its form regardless of its function in the relative clause.

relative clause

Here are the people *whose* car was stolen.

antecedent   possessive modifying *car*

Look at the house *whose* roof was fixed.

antecedent   possessive modifying *roof*

IN GERMAN

The possessive modifier is always in the genitive case. The form used depends on the gender of the antecedent.

Singular	Genitive	
MASCULINE	dessen	
FEMININE	deren	*whose*
NEUTER	dessen	
Plural	deren	

300

Let's look at an example.

*Hans, **whose** alarm clock was broken, overslept.*
> 1. ANTECEDENT: Hans
> 2. NUMBER & GENDER: *Hans* is masculine singular.
> 3. SELECTION: **dessen**

Hans, **dessen** Wecker kaputt war, hat sich verschlafen.

SUMMARY OF RELATIVE PRONOUNS

310

Here is a chart you can use as reference.

Function in Relative Clause	Antecedent Singular			Antecedent Plural
	MASCULINE	**FEMININE**	**NEUTER**	
NOMINATIVE	der	die	das	die
ACCUSATIVE	den	die	das	die
DATIVE	dem	der	dem	denen
GENITIVE	dessen	deren	dessen	deren

RELATIVE PRONOUNS WITHOUT ANTECEDENTS

320

There are relative pronouns that refer to an antecedent that has not been expressed or to an entire idea.

IN ENGLISH

There are two relative pronouns that can be used without an antecedent: *what* and *which*.

I don't know *what* happened.
> no antecedent

She didn't do well, *which* is too bad.
> antecedent an idea: the fact that she didn't do well

330

IN GERMAN

There is one relative pronoun that can be used without an antecedent: **was** *(which, what)*.

> entire clause as antecedent   relative clause

Anna hat uns eingeladen, **was** wir nett gefunden haben.
*Anna invited us all, **which** we found nice.*

Your textbook may give you examples of other instances that require the use of **was** as a relative pronoun.

Pattern

To help you remember the forms of the relative pronouns, look for similarities with another part of speech. Compare relative pronouns with definite articles.

RELATIVE PRONOUNS

	masc.	fem.	neut.	pl.
nom.	der	die	das	die
acc.	den	die	das	die
dat.	dem	der	dem	denen
gen.	dessen	deren	dessen	deren

DEFINITE ARTICLES

	masc.	fem.	neut.	pl.
nom.	der	die	das	die
acc.	den	die	das	die
dat.	dem	der	dem	den
gen.	des	der	des	der

What are the similarities between relative pronouns and definite articles?

- nominative, accusative, and dative singular→ identical
- genitive and dative plural → same first 3 letters (**des-, der-, des-, der-**)

Practice

Write two sentences that use the same noun in each sentence. Underline the noun, label its gender, and identify its function (case) in each sentence. Then combine the two sentences, replacing one of the nouns with a relative pronoun. Pay attention to the function (case) of the relative pronoun and the verb placement in the relative clause.

> **Der Bus** ist spät.   der Bus: masc., subject → nom.
> Ich warte auf **den Bus**.   den Bus: masc., direct object → acc.
> **Der Bus**, auf **den** ich warte, ist spät.
>
> *The bus is late.*
> *I'm waiting **for the bus**.*
> *The bus (that) I'm waiting for is late.*

WHAT IS MEANT BY MOOD?

The word MOOD in the grammatical sense refers to forms of a
verb that indicate the attitude of the speaker toward what he
or she is saying. The word itself is a variation of the word
mode, meaning manner or way.

1

Verb forms are divided into moods, which, in turn, are
subdivided into one or more tenses. You will learn when to
use the various moods as you learn verbs and their tenses. As
a beginning student of German, you need to know the
names of the moods so that you will understand what your
textbook is referring to when it uses these terms.

IN ENGLISH

10

Verbs can be in one of three moods:

Indicative mood — The indicative mood is used to indicate
an action of the verb that really happens or is likely to
happen. This is the most common mood, and most of the
verb forms that you use in everyday conversation belong
to the indicative mood.

> Hans *studies* German.
> Gabi *was* here.
> We *will go*.

20

The indicative mood occurs in the present tense (see
p. 104), the past tense (see p. 113), and the future tense
(see p. 123).

Imperative mood — The imperative mood is used to
express a command. The imperative mood does not have
different tenses (see p. 100).

> Hans, *study* German now!
> Anja, *be* here on time!

Subjunctive mood — The subjunctive mood is used to
express a subjective attitude or opinion about the action
of the verb, a contrary-to-fact statement, or a wish (see
p. 157).

30

> The teacher recommended that Paul *do* the exercise.
> If she *were* here, we would go to the party.
> If only he *were* with us.

IN GERMAN

These same three moods exist and have their own special forms. As in English, the indicative is the most common mood; the imperative is used similarly in both languages; the subjunctive, however, is used much more frequently in German than in English.

40

WHAT IS THE SUBJUNCTIVE?

The **SUBJUNCTIVE** is the mood of the verb used to express   1
hypothetical or contrary-to-fact situations, in contrast to the
indicative mood that is used to express facts.

> I wish Axel *were* here.
>
> hypothetical (Axel is not here) → subjunctive
>
> If Axel *were* here, you could meet him.
>
> contrary-to-fact (Axel is not here) → subjunctive
>
> Axel *is* here.
>
> fact (Axel is here) → indicative   10

IN ENGLISH

The subjunctive verb form is difficult to recognize because
it is spelled like other tenses of the verb, the dictionary
form and the simple past tense (see *What is the Infinitive?*,
p. 29 and p. 113 in *What is the Past Tense?*).

INDICATIVE	SUBJUNCTIVE
He *reads* a lot.	The course requires that he *read* a lot.
indicative present *to read*	subjunctive (same as dictionary form) 20
I *am* in Boston right now.	I wish I *were* in Berlin.
indicative present *to be*	subjunctive (same as past tense)

The subjunctive occurs most commonly in three kinds of
sentences.

- *if-clause* of contrary-to-fact sentences — the subjunctive
  form of the verb *to be* (*were*) is used. The result clause
  uses *would* + infinitive.

>   if-clause   result clause   30
>
> If I *were* in Europe now, I would go to Berlin.
>
> subjunctive
> Contrary-to-fact: I am *not* in Europe.
>
>   result clause   if-clause
>
> Franz would run faster, if he *were* in shape.
>
> subjunctive
> Contrary-to-fact: Franz is *not* in shape.

- conclusion of wish-statements — the subjunctive form of the verb *to be* (*were*) is used. The wish-statement is in the indicative.

  I wish I *were* in Europe right now.
     indicative subjunctive

  Franz wishes he *were* in shape.
      indicative   subjunctive

- following expressions that ask, urge, demand, request or express necessity — the subjunctive form of any verb is used.

  She asked that I *come* to see her.
    request   subjunctive same as dictionary form

  It is necessary that he *study* a lot.
    demand   subjunctive same as dictionary form

IN GERMAN

As in English, German has two subjunctive forms: the SUB-JUNCTIVE **II** (so called because the form is based on the second principal part of the verb, i.e., the simple past) is discussed in this chapter. The other, less common subjunctive, the SUBJUNCTIVE **I** (so called because the form is based on the first principal part of the verb, i.e., the infinitive) is discussed in *What is Meant by Direct and Indirect Discourse?*, p. 167. The subjunctive II has a present and a past tense formed as follows:

PRESENT SUBJUNCTIVE II — the stem of the indicative past tense (**Präteritum**) of the verb + subjunctive endings.

- **regular (weak) verbs** — the indicative past and the subjunctive II forms are identical.

  INFINITIVE: sagen *(to say)*
  INDICATIVE PAST TENSE: sagte *(I said)*
  PAST STEM: sagt-

INDICATIVE PAST	PRESENT SUBJUNCTIVE II
Du **sagtest**...	Wenn du **sagtest**...
Er **sagte**...	Wenn er **sagte**...
*You **said**...*	*If you **were** to say...*
*He **said**...*	*If he **were** to say...*

- **irregular (strong) verbs** — the stem vowels **a**, **o** and **u** of the indicative past add an umlaut. Note the addition of the letter **-e-** in the subjunctive endings.

INFINITIVE: kommen *(to come)*
INDICATIVE PAST TENSE: kam *(I came)*
PAST STEM (+ UMLAUT): käm-

INDICATIVE PAST	PRESENT SUBJUNCTIVE II	
ich kam	ich käme	*I came, I would come*
du kamst	du kämest	*you* etc.
er kam	er käme	
wir kamen	wir kämen	
ihr kamt	ihr kämet	
Sie kamen	Sie kämen	

PAST SUBJUNCTIVE II — the auxiliary verb **haben** *(to have)* or **sein** *(to be)* in the subjunctive II + the past participle of the main verb (see *What is a Participle?*, p. 116). This tense is often used to talk about things in the past we wish we had done differently.

Ich **hätte** das Buch **gekauft**, wenn ich es **gefunden hätte**.

past subjunctive   past subjunctive

*I **would have bought** the book if I **had found** it.*

Wenn wir nur früher **gekommen wären**!

past subjunctive

*If only we **had come** earlier!*

Consult your textbook for a detailed explanation of the subjunctive II forms, including exceptions.

THE WÜRDE-CONSTRUCTION

In spoken German, and increasingly in written German, the subjunctive II forms of the main verb are often replaced with the present subjunctive II form of **werden** *(to become)* + the infinitive of the main verb, a structure similar to the English structure *would* + the infinitive of the main verb.

ich **würde** kommen	*I would come*
du **würdest** kommen	*you would come*
er, sie, es **würde** kommen	*he, she, it would come*
wir **würden** kommen	*we would come*
ihr **würdet** kommen	*you would come*
sie, Sie **würden** kommen	*they, you would come*

Let's look at two examples.

Ich **würde gehen**, wenn ich Zeit hätte.
*I **would go** if I had time.*

Sie **würden** dich **einladen**, wenn sie könnten.
*They **would invite** you if they could.*

Usage of the subjunctive II or würde-construction

The subjunctive II or the **würde**-construction is commonly used in three kinds of sentences.

- *if*-clause and result clause of contrary-to-fact sentences — Unlike English where the subjunctive is used in the *if*-clause and the verb in the result clause uses *would* + infinitive, in German, the subjunctive II or **würde**-construction can be used in either or both clauses.

  *If she **were** here, I **would be** happy.*

  subjunctive   *would* + infinitive

  Wenn sie hier **wäre**, dann **wäre** ich glücklich.

  subjunctive   subjunctive

  *If it **were to rain**, I **would be** sad.*

  subjunctive   *would*
  + infinitive   + infinitive

  Wenn es **regnen würde**, dann **wäre** ich traurig.

  würde-construction   subjunctive

- both clauses of wish-statements — Unlike English where the subjunctive is only used in the result clause of the wish-statement, in German, the subjunctive II is used in both the wish-statement and in the conclusion.

  *I **wish** she **were** here!*

  indicative   subjunctive

  Ich **wünschte**, sie **wäre** doch hier!

  subjunctive   subjunctive

  *She **wishes** she **had** more time!*

  indicative   subjunctive

  Sie **wünschte**, sie **hätte** mehr Zeit!

  subjunctive   subjunctive

- to form polite requests — Just as English uses the construction *would* or *could* + the infinitive to make polite requests, German uses the verbs **werden** *(to become)* and modals, such as **können** *(to be able to)*, in the subjunctive II + the infinitive.

  __Could__ you __do__ me a favor?

  could   infinitive

  Könntest du mir einen Gefallen **tun**?

  subjunctive   infinitive

Would you please open the door?
   | |
  would   infinitive

Würden Sie bitte die Tür **aufmachen?**
   | |
 subjunctive   infinitive

- the auxiliary verbs **haben** *(to have)*, **sein** *(to be)*, and the modal verbs do not use the **würde**-construction. For these verbs, always use the one-word subjunctive II forms (see p. 106 in *What is an Auxiliary Verb?*). ¹⁷⁰

CAREFUL — Pay attention to the use of the umlaut in subjunctive II forms. It not only affects pronunciation, but completely changes the meaning of the sentence. Notice how the umlauted vowel can change the verb tense or mood.

INDICATIVE PAST	SUBJUNCTIVE II
Wir **waren gegangen.**	Wir **wären gegangen.**
We had gone.	*We would have gone.*
Ich **konnte schwimmen.**	Ich **könnte schwimmen.**
I was able to swim.	*I would be able to swim.*

180

CHAPTER

WHAT IS MEANT BY ACTIVE
AND PASSIVE VOICE?

VOICE in the grammatical sense refers to the relationship between the verb and its subject. There are two voices, the **ACTIVE VOICE** and the **PASSIVE VOICE**.

Active voice — A sentence is said to be in the active voice when the subject is the performer of the action of the verb. In this instance, the verb is called an **ACTIVE VERB**.

> The teacher prepares the exam.
> S   V   DO

> Axel ate an apple.
> S   V   DO

> Lightning has struck the tree.
> S   V   DO

In these examples the subject (S) performs the action of the verb (V) and the direct object (DO) is the receiver of the action (see *What is a Subject?*, p. 41 and *What is an Object?*, p. 53).

Passive voice — A sentence is said to be in the passive voice when the subject receives the action of the verb. In this instance, the verb is called a **PASSIVE VERB**.

> The exam is prepared by the teacher.
> S   V   agent

> The apple was eaten by Axel.
> S   V   agent

> The tree has been struck by lightning.
> S   V   agent

In these examples, the subject receives the action of the verb. The performer of the action, if it is mentioned, is introduced by the word "by" and is called the **AGENT**.

IN ENGLISH

The passive voice is expressed by the verb *to be* conjugated in the appropriate tense + the past participle of the main verb (see p. 119). The tense of the passive sentence is indicated by the tense of the verb *to be*.

The exam *is* prepared by the teacher.
|
present

The exam *was* prepared by the teacher.
|
past

The exam *will be* prepared by the teacher.
└─┬─┘
future

In English only transitive verbs, i.e., verbs that can have a direct object, can be used in the passive voice.

MAKING AN ACTIVE SENTENCE PASSIVE

The steps to change an active sentence into a passive one are as follows.

1. The direct object of the active sentence becomes the subject of the passive sentence.

   ACTIVE   The mechanic is repairing *the car.*
   |
   direct object

   PASSIVE   *The car* is repaired by the mechanic.
   |
   subject

2. The tense of the verb of the active sentence is reflected in the tense of the verb *to be* in the passive sentence.

   ACTIVE   The mechanic *repairs* the car.
   |
   present

   PASSIVE   The car *is* repaired by the mechanic.
   |
   present

   ACTIVE   The mechanic *has repaired* the car.
   └───┬───┘
   present perfect

   PASSIVE   The car *has been* repaired by the mechanic.
   └──┬──┘
   present perfect

3. The subject of the active sentence becomes the agent of the passive sentence or the agent is omitted.

   ACTIVE   *The mechanic* is repairing the car.
   |
   subject

   PASSIVE   The car is being repaired *by the mechanic.*
   |
   agent

   The car is being repaired.
   |
   no agent

IN GERMAN

Unlike English, the passive voice is used extensively in German, particularly in formal writing. It is formed by the verb **werden** *(to become)* conjugated in the appropriate tense + the past participle of the main verb. The form of **werden** must agree in number with the new subject. The tense of passive sentences is indicated by the tense of the verb **werden**.

> Der Roman **wird** gelesen.
> |
> present
> *The novel **is being** read.*

> Der Roman **wurde** gelesen.
> |
> simple past
> *The novel **was (being)** read.*

> Der Roman **wird** gelesen **werden**.
> |_____|
> future
> *The novel **will be** read.*

> Der Roman **ist** gelesen **worden**.
> |_____|
> perfect
> *The novel **was (has been)** read.*

> Der Roman **war** gelesen **worden**.
> |_____|
> past perfect
> *The novel **had been** read.*

As you can see in the last two examples, in passive sentences the perfect and past perfect tenses drop the **ge-** of the past participle of **werden: geworden → worden**.

MAKING AN ACTIVE SENTENCE PASSIVE

To change an active sentence into passive in German, you can follow the same steps as for English on p. 163. You will also have to change the case of the words to reflect their new function in the passive sentence.

SUBJECT — The accusative object of an active sentence becomes the nominative subject of the passive sentence.

> ACTIVE   *The woman reads **the novel.***
> Die Frau liest **den Roman.**
> |_____|
> accusative

> PASSIVE   ***The novel** is read by the woman.*
> **Der Roman** wird von der Frau gelesen.
> |_____|
> nominative

ACTIVE   *Ilse sings **such songs**.*
          Ilse singt **solche Lieder**.
          └───────┬───────┘
               accusative

PASSIVE   ***Such songs** are sung by Ilse.*
          Solche Lieder werden von Ilse gesungen.
          └──────┬──────┘
              nominative

AGENT — If the agent is mentioned, it is expressed differently depending on whether it refers to a person or not.

- **person** — If the nominative subject of an active sentence is a person, it is expressed by **von** + dative object in a passive sentence.

  ACTIVE   ***Many people** heard the speech.*
            Viele Leute hörten die Rede.
            └──────┬──────┘
               nominative

  PASSIVE   *The speech was heard **by many people**.*
            Die Rede wurde **von vielen Leuten** gehört.
            └──────────┬──────────┘
                   dative

- **not a person** — If the nominative subject of an active sentence is not a person, it is expressed by **durch** + accusative object in a passive sentence.

  ACTIVE   *Fire has destroyed the building.*
            Feuer hat das Gebäude zerstört.
            │
            nominative

  PASSIVE   *The building was destroyed **by the fire**.*
            Das Gebäude ist **durch das Feuer** zerstört worden.
            └──────────┬──────────┘
                   accusative

IMPERSONAL PASSIVES

Unlike English, German sometimes uses intransitive verbs, verbs that cannot have a direct object, in the passive voice. Such constructions are called **IMPERSONAL PASSIVES**, because the verb expresses an activity with no reference to a personal subject. The emphasis is on the activity, rather than on who is doing it. In place of a personal subject, the impersonal pronoun **es** is introduced as the formal subject of the sentence. The auxiliary **werden** is conjugated to agree with **es**.

ACTIVE   Die Kinder **schlafen** hier.
          *The children **are sleeping** here.*

PASSIVE   **Es wird** hier **geschlafen**.
          [word-for-word: it is here slept]

If you change a sentence that has only a dative object from active to passive, the object remains in the dative case instead of becoming the subject of the passive sentence. The impersonal subject **es** may be added, and consequently changing the word order.

170

ACTIVE   Man dankt **ihm**.

                 dative object
*One thanks **him**.*

PASSIVE   **Ihm** wird gedankt.
            Es wird **ihm** gedankt.

               dative subject
He is thanked.

180

ACTIVE   Sie glaubten **den Kindern** nicht.

                  dative object
*They didn't believe **the children**.*

PASSIVE   **Den Kindern** wurde nicht geglaubt.
            Es wurde **den Kindern** nicht geglaubt.

               dative subject
***The children** were not believed.*

Note that many impersonal passives in German cannot be translated word-for-word into English. Your textbook will show you several alternatives to the passive construction in German.

WHAT IS MEANT BY DIRECT AND INDIRECT DISCOURSE?

In **DIRECT DISCOURSE** a statement is made directly between a speaker and a listener. Direct discourse is usually set in quotation marks.

> Inge said, "I am going to Berlin."
> Axel asked, "What will you do in Berlin?"

In **INDIRECT (REPORTED) DISCOURSE** another person's statement is transmitted without quoting their words directly.

> Inge said she was going to Berlin.
> Axel asked what she would do in Berlin.

While indirect discourse reproduces the substance of the message, it cannot reproduce the statement word-for-word.

IN ENGLISH

When direct discourse is changed to indirect discourse some words, such as pronouns and possessive adjectives, must be changed to reflect the change of speaker. There is also a shift in tense.

> DIRECT DISCOURSE   Inge said, "*I am going* to Berlin."
>   PRONOUNS: I → she
>   TENSE: am going (present) → was going (past)
> INDIRECT DISCOURSE   Inge said *she was going* to Berlin.
>
> DIRECT DISCOURSE   Inge said, "*I was* in Berlin with *my* sister."
>   PRONOUNS: I → she
>   POSSESSIVE ADJECTIVE: my → her
>   TENSE: was (past) → had been (past perfect)
> INDIRECT DISCOURSE   Inge said *she had been* in Berlin with *her* sister.

IN GERMAN

As in English, when direct discourse is changed to indirect discourse the pronouns used in the original statement are changed. Unlike English where there is only a shift in tense, in German there is a shift in mood (see *What is Meant by Mood?*, p. 155). In direct discourse the verb is in the indicative, in indirect discourse the verb is in the **SUBJUNCTIVE I** (so called because the form is based on the first principal part of the verb, i.e., the infinitive).

The subjunctive I has a present and a past tense.

PRESENT SUBJUNCTIVE I OF REGULAR (WEAK) AND IRREGULAR (STRONG) VERBS → the stem of the infinitive + the subjunctive endings. Note that vowel changes to stem-changing verbs do not apply here.

INFINITIVE: fahren *(to drive)*
STEM: fahr-

INDICATIVE PRESENT	PRESENT SUBJUNCTIVE I
ich fahre	ich fahre
du fährst	du fahrest
er fährt	er fahre
wir fahren	wir fahren
ihr fahrt	ihr fahret
Sie fahren	Sie fahren

Here is an example.

DIRECT DISCOURSE Ingrid sagte, "Ich **fahre** nach Berlin."

present indicative

*Ingrid said, "I **am going** to Berlin."*
PRONOUN: I (**ich**) → she (**sie**)
MOOD: I am going (**ich fahre** — indicative) → she was going (**sie fahre** — subjunctive I)

INDIRECT DISCOURSE Ingrid sagte, sie **fahre** nach Berlin.

subjunctive I present
*Ingrid said she **was going** to Berlin.*

PAST SUBJUNCTIVE I → the subjunctive I form of the helping verb **haben** *(to have)* or **sein** *(to be)* + the past participle of the main verb.

DIRECT DISCOURSE Ingrid sagte, "Ich **war** in Berlin."

simple past indicative

*Ingrid said, "I **was** in Berlin."*
PRONOUN: I (**ich**) → she (**sie**)
MOOD: I was (**ich war** — indicative) → she had been (**sei gewesen** — subjunctive I)

IINDIRECT DISCOURSE Ingrid sagte, sie **sei** in Berlin **gewesen**.

subjunctive I past
*Ingrid said she **had been** in Berlin.*

The subjunctive I is used primarily in written and spoken German news reporting. In casual conversation, however, it is often replaced by the subjunctive II (see p. 158). Your German textbook will explain in greater detail the formation and use of the subjunctive in indirect discourse.